PRIMA'S OFFICIAL STRATEGY GUIDE
JOE GRANT BELL

Prima Games
A Division of Random House, Inc.
3000 Lava Ridge Court
Roseville, CA 95661
(800) 733-3000
www.primagames.com

Associate Product Manager: Christy L. Curtis

Project Editor: Matt Sumpter

Design & Layout: Scott Watanabe

TABLE OF CONTENTS

Welcome to *PlanetSide* 4

Chapter 1: Introduction to *PlanetSide* 6

Auraxis™ 6

Vanu Technology 6

Collapse of the Wormhole 7

The Empires 7

Terran Republic 7

Vanu Sovereignty 8

New Conglomerate 8

Game Flow 9

Game Concepts 9

Constant Battle 9

Massive Scale 10

Teamwork 10

Organizational Tools 10

Chapter 2: Weapons 11

Weapon Stats 11

Blades 11

Chainblade (TR) 12

MAG Cutter (NC) 12

Forceblade (VS) 12

Standard Weapons 13

AMP (Automatic Machine Pistol)
(Common Pool) 13

Beamer (VS) 13

Repeater (TR) 14

MAG Scatter Pistol (NC) 14

Suppressor (Common Pool) 15

Medium Assault Weapons 16

Sweeper (Common Pool) 16

Punisher (Common Pool) 17

Pulsar (VS) 17

Cycler (TR) 18

Gauss Rifle (NC) 18

Heavy Assault Weapons 19

Lasher (VS) 19

Mini-Chaingun (TR) 20

Jackhammer (NC) 20

Anti-Vehicle Weapons 21

Lancer (VS) 21

Striker (TR) 22

Phoenix (NC) 22

Sniping Weapons 23

Bolt Driver (Common Pool) 23

Special Assault Weapons 23

Decimator (Common Pool) 24

Rocklet Rifle (Common Pool) 24

Thumper (Common Pool) 25

MAX Weapons 25

Anti-Personnel MAX Weapons 25

Anti-Vehicle MAX Weapons 27

Anti-Aircraft MAX Weapons 28

Grenades, Engineer Explosives,
and Turrets 29

Grenades (Common Pool) 29

Engineers' Explosives (Common Pool) . . 30

Turrets (Common Pool) 31

Summary 31

Chapter 3: Armor 32

Armor in Focus 32

Explanation of Values 32

Standard Exosuit 33

Agile Exosuit 34

Reinforced Battle Armor 36

Infiltration Suit 37

MAX Armor 38

General MAX Characteristics 40

Faction Variations 41

Specific MAX Types 42

Final Analysis 43

Chapter 4: Vehicles .44

Vehicle Stats and Characteristics 44

Utility Vehicles 45

AMS (Advanced Mobile Station) 45

ANT (Advanced Nanite Transport) 46

Four-Wheeled Cycles 47

Assault Basilisk .47

Wraith 48

Assault Buggies 48

Harasser 49

Marauder (TR) 50

Enforcer (NC) 51

Thresher (VS) 52

Tanks 53

Lightning 53

Prowler (TR) 54

Vanguard (NC) 55

MagRider (VS) 56

Land Transports 57

Deliverer 57

Sunderer 58

Air Units 59

Mosquito 59

Reaver 60

Galaxy 61

Chapter 5: How Things Work—Terminals,
Gadgets, and Emplaced Devices 62

Base Objects 62

Terminals 62

Other Facility Devices 67

NTU Silo 70

Handheld Devices .71

Remote Electronics Kit (REK) 71

Medkit 71

Medical Applicator 72

Body Armor Nano Kit (Bank) 72

Nano Dispenser .73

Command Uplink Device 73

Engineer Devices 73

Motion Sensors .74

Spitfire Turrets 75

HE Mines 76

Boomer HE 77

Distance and SOI (Sphere of Influence)
Mechanics 77

Player Communication Range 78

Range of Game-Generated Messages . .78

Receiving Experience from
Squad Actions 79

Deploying Items .79

Hacking 79

Effects of Hacking 80

What You Can Hack 80

Hack Speed 80

Chapter 6: Auraxis™ 82

Servers 82

World Map and Overview 83

Reading the In-Game Map (Global View) .84

Reading the In-Game Map (Tactical View) 84

The Proximity Map 85

What the Proximity Map Shows 85

Zoom Levels and Details
Sanctuaries 86

New Conglomerate Sanctuary (map) . . .86

Terran Republic Sanctuary (map) 87

Vanu Sovereignty Sactuary (map) 87

Detail of Central Building Cluster (all
Sanctuaries map) 88

Respawning Facilities 89

Virtual Training Center 89

Virtual Reality Driving Zone (map) 90

HART (High Altitude Rapid Transport)
Shuttle Buildings 91

Meeting Hall 92

Land Vehicle Terminals 92

Air Vehicle Terminals 93

Warp Gates 93

Battle Continents 93

Amerish (map) .94

Ceryshen (map) .95

Cyssor (map) 96

Esamir (map) 97

Forseral (map) 98

Hossin (map) 99

Ishundar (map) .100

Oshur (map) 101

Searhus (map) .102

Solsar (map) 103

Facilities 104

A Note on Facilites and ANTs 104

AMP Stations .105

Bio Labs 107

DropShip Centers 109

Interlink Facilities 111

Tech Plants 113

Towers 115

Transportation .115

Warp Gates 115

HART (High Altitude Rapid Transport)
Shuttle 116

Deconstruction 116

Recall to Sanctuary 117

Suicide Solution 117

Instant Action .117

Planet-Wide Game Systems 118

Empire Balance 118

Experience Point bonuses and
Penalties 119

Hit Point (Health) Penalties 119

Grief System 119

Chapter 7: Certifications, Implants, and
Character Development 121

Overview of Character Planning 121

Multiple Characters 122

BEPs and Battle Rank 122

Battle Rank Breakdown 123

Gaining Experience 124

Certifications 124

Weapon Certifications 125

Armor Certifications 128

Vehicle Certifications 131

Equipment Certifications 136

Implants 138

Advanced Regeneration 139

Advanced Targeting 139

Audio Amplifier 139

Darklight Vision 140

Melee Booster 140

Personal Shield 140

Range Magnifier 141

Second Wind 141

Silent Run 141

Surge 142

CEPs and Command Rank 142

Command Rank 1 Benefits 143

Command Rank 2 Benefits 144

Command Rank 3 Benefits 144

Command Rank 4 Benefits 145

Command Rank 5 Benefits 146

Chapter 8: Combat 147

Decide Whether to Fight 147

Understand the Weapon and Armor
Hierarchies 147

Abandon Hopeless Situations 148

Be Effective Without Fighting 149

Avoid Combat Zones 149

Firing Weapons 149

Pick the Right Weapon 150

Where to Aim .150

Cone-of-Fire Considerations 151

Combat Movement and Tactics 153

Constant Running: Not in Vogue 153

Crouch But Don't Crawl 153

Use Cover 154

Run Around in Close Combat 155

Zoom In While Traveling 155

Watch Your Stamina 155

Putting it all Together 156

Fighting Heavier Opponents 156

Fighting Lighter Opponents 157

Fighting Evenly Matched Opponents . .158

Using Health and Defensive
Advantages 159

Keep Your Focus 159

Fighting in and Against Vehicles 160

When a Vehicle Shows Up, and
You're on Foot .160

When Facing Mixed Groups of
Vehicles and Infantry 162

Driving a Combat Vehicle 162

Team Fighting Techniques 163

Stick Together—But Not Too Together 163

Maintain Mixed Groups 164

Have Anti-Vehicle and Anti-Personnel
Weapons 165

Step Back When Injured 166

Flank If Possible 166

Learn Your Squad 166

Keep Your Eyes Open 167

Chapter 9: Team Strategy 168

Getting Organized 168

You Need Help! 169

Squads and Outfits 169

Join or Create? 171

Finding the Group for You 172

Base Assault 101 172

Choosing a Target 173

Reconnaissance 174

Planning and Gathering 175

Vehicle and Personnel Deployment . . .176

Neutralizing Exterior Forces 177

Base Entry 178

Neutralizing Interior Forces 178

Hacking the Command Console 179

Defending During the Capture Period .180

Re-Equipping, Deploying
Infrastructure, and Leaving Guards . . .181

Base Defense 101 181

Squads Are Still Important 182

Deploy Infrastructure 182

Watch the Big Map; Watch the
Proximity Map 182

Focus on the Exterior 183

Use Wall Turrets 184

Use Vehicles—Especially AMSes 184

Call for Help 185

Hunt Enemy Mines 185

Fall Back on the Interior 186

Stealth Works for Re-Hacks! 186

Chapter 10: Finding a Role 187

A Few Words About Roles 187

MAXes 188

Tasks for the Anti-Infantry MAX 188

Tasks for the Anti-Vehicle MAX 189

Tasks for the Anti-Air MAX 191

General Infantry .192

Anti-Vehicle Fighters 192

Anti-Personnel Fighters 192

Support Roles 193

Transport or Support Driver 193

Medic 194

Engineer 194

Scout 196

Hacker 197

Specialized Combat Roles 197

Sniper 197

Assault Vehicle Driver 198

Gunner 199

Stealth Assassin 199

Useful Role Combinations 200

   Anti-Vehicle and Anti-Personnel
   Fighter 200

   Combat Engineer 201

   Stealth Hacker and MAX 201

   Stealth Engineer 202

   Multiple Vehicle Specialist 202

   More Combinations 202

Chapter 11: Advanced Play 203

   The Ideal Squad? 203

   Poor Squad Composition: Amusing,
   But Not Helpful 203

   Squad Composition: A Good Model . . .204

   Specialized Squads For
   Specialized Duty 205

   Reality Interferes 206

Things to Avoid .206

   Avoiding Pointless Battles 206

   The Lonely Sniper 207

   The Compressed Defense 208

The All-Important AMS 208

   Demand an AMS 209

   Hiding an AMS 209

   Protecting an AMS 210

   You Can Never Have Too
   Many AMSes .211

   How Close is Too Close? 212

NTU Levels and Assaults 212

Dealing with Limited Attack Resources . .213

   Take Nearby Towers 213

   Load up on Anti-Vehicle Weapons 213

   Trash the Case as Quickly as Possible .214

   Move in Packs 214

Maximize Deployable Power 214

   Use Cover 215

   Aim High 215

   Use Camouflage 215

   Group Explosives with Other Items 216

Stealth Techniques 216

   Patience! 217

   Avoid Obvious Places 217

   Don't Panic 218

   Let Your Darklight Shine 218

   Know When to Quit 218

Continued Improvement 219

   Study Your Failures 219

   Team Up with the Best 219

   Acknowledge Your Limitations 220

WELCOME TO PLANETSIDE

Welcome to *PlanetSide*: Prima's Official Strategy Guide!

At first glance, *PlanetSide* may seem like a natural evolution of first-person shooters and massively multiplayer role-playing games. When you dig below the surface, you'll find truly radical ideas. Can an action game work in a persistent, always-on environment? Will it continue to interest you, even though there's no clear-cut beginning or end? Will the emphasis on team play really work?

The answer is an emphatic "Yes!" on all counts. The *PlanetSide* team has captured the excitement and tension of battle on a global scale, without sacrificing the experience for individual players. The tough part is learning to be effective in this new—and competitive— environment.

This book is both an introduction and a companion to *PlanetSide*. It gets you started on the right track and provides inside information on all the guns, gadgets, vehicles, and locations that you must become familiar with in the process of mastering the game. By the time you're done reading, you'll have a big advantage over other newcomers—and after putting its information and strategies into practice, you'll soon rank among *PlanetSide*'s accomplished veterans.

Here's a quick look at the book's structure:

- Chapter 1 is an extension of this introduction, providing background information and setting the stage for the rest of the book.
- Chapter 2 breaks down *PlanetSide*'s myriad weapons, comparing strengths and weaknesses, and recommends guns for every task.
- Chapter 3 discusses armor types.
- Chapter 4 investigates vehicles and recommends strategies for getting the most from them.
- Chapter 5 explains various gadgets and devices, from handheld tools to Vehicle Terminals and facility Generators.
- Chapter 6 is an overview of the game world, Auraxis™. It looks at Sanctuaries, Battle Continents, and the facilities that are your primary objectives.
- Chapter 7 is all about character development, covering topics such as Certifications, Battle Ranks, Command Ranks, and Implants.
- Chapter 8 provides tactics and techniques for the heart of the game: combat.
- Chapter 9 suggests strategies for accomplishing common team goals, such as assaulting or defending an installation.
- Chapter 10 recommends roles for your character, such as scout, transport driver, or stealth assassin.
- Chapter 11 is a compendium of tips for improving your game.

Feel free to either read the book straight through or use it as a reference, reading only the sections that interest you. Our recommendation is to break up your reading with a few play sessions; you'll remember more, and everything will make more sense if you have some in-game experiences to draw upon.

This book is both an introduction and a companion to *PlanetSide*. It gets you started on the right track and provides inside information on all the guns, gadgets, vehicles, and locations that you must become familiar with in the process of mastering the game. By the time you're done reading, you'll have a big advantage over other newcomers—and after putting its information and strategies into practice, you'll soon rank among *PlanetSide*'s accomplished veterans. Please keep in mind that the information in this book was correct at the time of printing. However, *PlanetSide* is an ever-changing world and all of this information is subject to change at any time.

With that said, let's move on to the good stuff!

ACKNOWLEDGMENTS

Thanks to the following people for making this book a reality:

Michael Lustenberger

Lisa Leyba

Terrence Yee

Danny Han

Ari Zgliniec

Christy Curtis

Matt Sumpter

CHAPTER 1: INTRODUCTION TO PLANETSIDE

This chapter is a quick introduction to *PlanetSide*. It outlines the world and its three Empires, touches on the concepts that make the game unique, and previews what to expect when you first touch down on Auraxis™.

You can skip this stuff if you want to get right to the hard strategy, but we recommend reviewing it so you get the basic concepts straight.

AURAXIS™

The Terran Republic, an intergalactic hegemony that dictated all human affairs for thousands of years, maintained its rule through expansion and colonization. In recent years it discovered a new wormhole, and just beyond that wormhole was an intriguing planet named Auraxis™.

An expeditionary force was sent through the wormhole to explore and colonize Auraxis™. The force established orbital platforms above the planet, bases on the planet itself, and a wide array of facilities on Auraxis™'s 10 large continents.

VANU TECHNOLOGY

Artifacts of an extremely powerful and advanced alien race (dubbed the Vanu) were discovered during colonization. There was no trace of the Vanu themselves, but the technology eventually revealed its secrets to human scientists.

The most astounding technology gleaned from these artifacts was rebirthing, the ability to bind a person's genetic pattern to a matrix and recall it in the event of death. Because of this technology, there was no longer any need to fear accidental or violent death.

Another major technological advance was the development of Warp Gates, which allow instantaneous transport between continents.

COLLAPSE OF THE WORMHOLE

The wormhole collapsed during the last stages of colonization, cutting off the colonists from the rest of the Terran Republic. Because there was no central government on Auraxis™ to impose its will, dissidents arose, emboldened by the virtual immortality offered by rebirthing. Dissension soon led to fighting, and eventually the colonists split into three distinct factions that became known as Empires. A full-scale war for control of Auraxis™ was set in motion—a strange war, in which death was not permanent.

THE EMPIRES

The three Empires of Auraxis™ each possess a single Sanctuary, which is an inviolate base that no other Empire may attack. From these Sanctuaries, each Empire stages attacks in an attempt to control Auraxis™'s 10 continents.

TERRAN REPUBLIC

The Terran Republic consists of loyalists who still support the status quo. To them, the collapse of the wormhole is no excuse for anarchy and chaos. Members of the other two Empires are nothing more than traitors and deserters.

Members of the Terran Republic believe that the end always justifies the means. If the end result is peace and order, it's acceptable to cut a few corners along the way—by restricting personal liberty, for example. Fear and oppression are the most effective tools for imposing law.

The Terran Republic's weapons fire faster than those of the other Empires, and their vehicles are heavier and better-armored.

VANU SOVEREIGNTY

The Vanu Sovereignty believes in researching and exploiting Vanu technology as much as possible. If technology can be used to geneti- cally re-engineer the human race, thus elimi- nating flaws and paving the way to a more enlightened state, the Vanu Sovereignty will attempt it.

The Vanu Sovereignty dismisses the Terran Republic as a monolithic relic of humankind's enduring barbarity, and the New Conglomerate is seen as a loose collection of misguided rabble.

Vanu Sovereignty weapons tend to have a slower rate of fire than those of the Terran Republic and less punch than New Conglomerate weaponry, but they possess a built-in armor- piercing ability that levels the playing field. Also, while Vanu weapons and vehicles generally don't have the raw power of other Empires' engines of war, they often have unique features (such as their hover-vehicles' ability to cross water) that other Empires cannot duplicate.

NEW CONGLOMERATE

The New Conglomerate is in direct opposition to the Terran Republic. Its goal is freedom for the individual: freedom from the Terran Republic's oppression, and freedom from the Vanu Sovereignty's mad-scientist schemes. Members of the New Conglomerate see themselves as freedom fighters, liberating humanity from the shackles of ages.

New Conglomerate weapons and vehicles hit harder than comparable devices from the other Empires. They pack all their power into massive, discrete shots, rather than firing a fast stream of lead. This emphasis encourages accuracy over rapid fire and is particularly deadly against lightly armored targets.

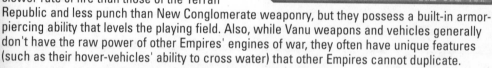

GAME FLOW

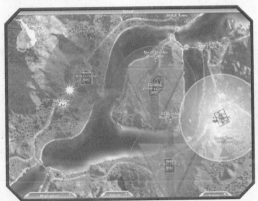

Your goal in *PlanetSide* is to acquire (and defend) territory for your Empire. Territory is acquired by capturing the many facilities (also known as bases or installations) scattered across each Battle Continent.

If your Empire gains control of every single facility on a Battle Continent, you'll achieve a "continent lock," which prevents enemies from entering that continent through Warp Gates. The only way to attack a locked continent is via the HART (High Altitude Rapid Transport) shuttle, which drops players onto a particular continent in individual Drop Pods.

In practice, you won't be gobbling up whole continents at a time. Instead, your activities in a typical play session will revolve around attacking or defending a handful of facilities.

GAME CONCEPTS

Several important characteristics set *PlanetSide* apart from other games. Here's a quick overview of the most significant.

CONSTANT BATTLE

Battles rage across Auraxis™ 24 hours a day, seven days a week, and 365 days a year. (Save, of course, for unexpected network events and scheduled maintenance!)

Because of this, expect the game world to change —sometimes a lot—between when you log off and when you log on again the next day.

The continuous nature of the game allows you to play whenever you want, but if you develop friendships with other players (and you probably will), you'll take your friends' schedules into consideration. If your favorite teammates log in at a particular time, you'll probably want to be in the game at that time as well.

MASSIVE SCALE

Auraxis™ is a huge game world. Its 10 continents are massive in their own right; it is not practical, for example, to run to a facility on the other side of a continent. It can be done, but it takes far too long to be useful. Vehicles are necessary.

This large battlefield scale has repercussions on gameplay. Even when the game is packed with players, you'll be able to find a low-traffic (or even deserted) base for infiltration or subterfuge.

TEAMWORK

Many games have attempted to force teamwork, and many have failed or only partially succeeded. *PlanetSide* was built as a team game from the ground up.

Success in *PlanetSide* is extremely difficult if you play it as a strictly solo endeavor. *PlanetSide* encourages you to cooperate with allies. Chapter nine explores the team aspect of the game.

ORGANIZATIONAL TOOLS

Teamwork is a noble ideal, but without the right game structure and in-game tools, it becomes nightmarishly hard to coordinate. *PlanetSide* provides not only mechanisms that reward teamwork but also useful tools that let you easily find teammates, connect with them, keep track of them, and cooperate with them.

Teamwork still requires a bit of effort, but the rewards are tangible. Success in the game depends partially on personal ability and partially on the ability and performance of your friends. As a result, despite the fact that it's an action game, reflexes alone play a smaller role in *PlanetSide* success than you might think.

CHAPTER 2: WEAPONS

This chapter examines and compares *PlanetSide*'s wide assortment of handheld and MAX-mounted weapons. (Vehicle-based weapons are discussed in chapter 4.)

Picking the right weapons is a multi-step process. The first step is to read this chapter and figure out which guns are most appropriate for the role you're playing. A base crasher needs strong anti-personnel weapons, while an outdoor defender might specialize in sniper weapons or perhaps anti-vehicle weapons.

Once you've got a handle on each weapon's abilities, you're ready to pick the right gun for any job. However, there are so many weapons—many of which have overlapping functionality—that there's a lot of room for personal preference. By testing weapons in the field and noting which ones you like best, you'll eventually narrow down the selection to a few guns that work well for you.

WEAPON STATS

Stats are provided for every weapon. Most of these stats are highly abstract, because the values are guaranteed to change as *PlanetSide* evolves and is tested by thousands of players.

The following stats are rated from 1 (worst) to 5 (best) for most weapons:

Rate of Fire: How fast the weapon can spit out ammo

Accuracy: Relative size of the weapon's cone of fire

Shot Power: How damaging the shots are, on average

Effective Range: How far the bullets travel

Ammo Amount: How much ammo this weapon holds

The following stats express the ammo type and the damage dealt to various targets:

Ammo Type: Type(s) of ammunition the weapon uses

Damage Type: This can be direct, explosive, or aggravated (burns)

Vs. Infantry: Amount of damage dealt to infantry, per shot

Vs. Vehicles: Amount of damage dealt to vehicles, per shot

Vs. Aircraft: Amount of damage dealt to aircraft, per shot

Weapons that fire multiple ammo types and weapons with multiple distinct firing modes have separate stats for each option.

BLADES

Each non-MAX armor type has a built-in blade weapon. These weapons are typically used as a last resort, though players in Infiltration Suits can use them as primary weapons—especially if they have the Melee Booster Implant.

CHAINBLADE (TR)

Ammo Type: —

Damage Type: Direct

Vs. Infantry: 25/50 (deactivated/activated)

Vs. Vehicles: —

Vs. Aircraft: —

This blade is the Terran Republic's weapon of last resort. It deals minimal damage at close range. The secondary fire mode activates loud but damage-enhancing teeth along the blade, for times when you're willing to trade stealth for power.

Frankly, we don't recommend blades for serious combat. They're always available to all armor types, and they're always at hand. Most characters will only pull out a blade when they're desperate.

The exception is a specialist using the Melee Booster Implant and an Infiltration Suit.

MAG CUTTER (NC)

Ammo Type: —

Damage Type: Direct

Vs. Infantry: 25/50 (deactivated/activated)

Vs. Vehicles: —

Vs. Aircraft: —

The New Conglomerate's MAG Cutter is a standard blade in its primary mode; it becomes a loud, magnetically charged vibrating blade in its secondary mode.

FORCEBLADE (VS)

Ammo Type: —

Damage Type: Direct

Vs. Infantry: 25/50 (deactivated/activated)

Vs. Vehicles: —

Vs. Aircraft: —

The Vanu Sovereignty's fallback knife is a standard blade in primary fire mode and a glowing, extra-damaging force weapon in secondary mode. Whereas the blade weapons of the other Empires trade noise for power, the Forceblade trades visibility for power.

STANDARD WEAPONS

Every new character has access to these weapons. As you might expect, they're all fairly limited—but they're serviceable, and some characters get lots of mileage out of them.

AMP (AUTOMATIC MACHINE PISTOL) (COMMON POOL)

Rate of Fire: 4

Accuracy: 2

Shot Power: 3

Effective Range: 1

Ammo Amount: 3

Ammo Type: 9mm standard

Damage Type: Direct

Vs. Infantry: 18

Vs. Vehicles: 3

Vs. Aircraft: 3

Ammo Type: 9mm AP (armor-piercing)

Damage Type: Direct

Vs. Infantry: 10

Vs. Vehicles: 8

Vs. Aircraft: 8

The AMP is a machine pistol with a good rate of fire but atrocious accuracy, especially at moderate to long range. It has an excellent rate of fire and a good ammo supply.

Like all pistols, the AMP is nearly worthless against vehicles. The armor-piercing ammo is best used against deployable devices, and static items at enemy bases.

This is an excellent weapon for assassin-types in Infiltration Suits. If you can get to point-blank range and unload on your target, you can deal excellent damage and score a kill on any non-MAX.

BEAMER (VS)

Rate of Fire: 2

Accuracy: 3

Shot Power: 3

Effective Range: 2

Ammo Amount: 2

Ammo Type: Energy cell—primary mode

Damage Type: Direct

Vs. Infantry: 18

Vs. Vehicles: 3

Vs. Aircraft: 3

Ammo Type: Energy cell—secondary (AP) mode

Damage Type: Direct

Vs. Infantry: 10

Vs. Vehicles: 8

Vs. Aircraft: 8

The Beamer pistol uses a single energy source to power both standard (anti-infantry) and armor-piercing modes. Armor-piercing mode is activated by the secondary fire button; it consumes twice the energy of standard shots.

The Beamer is inventory-friendly, thanks to its reliance on only a single ammo source.

This pistol has substantial recoil, so single shots are much more accurate than rapid fire. Overall, the weapon is slower to fire but more accurate at range than the AMP. Take the AMP if you specialize in short-range assassinations, but take the Beamer for a somewhat more versatile weapon, especially at range.

REPEATER (TR)

Rate of Fire: 3
Accuracy: 3
Shot Power: 3
Effective Range: 2
Ammo Amount: 2
Ammo Type: 9mm standard
Damage Type: Direct
Vs. Infantry: 18
Vs. Vehicles: 3
Vs. Aircraft: 3
Ammo Type: 9mm AP
Damage Type: Direct
Vs. Infantry: 10
Vs. Vehicles: 8
Vs. Aircraft: 8

The Repeater is a large-caliber pistol with reasonable accuracy. It's more effective than, say, the AMP or MAG Scatter Pistol at medium to long range. However, it lacks those pistols' up-close stopping power. The Repeater fires faster than the Beamer but lacks the Beamer's efficient all-in-one ammo source.

Once again, take the Repeater for a light general-use weapon, the AMP for close-range specialization.

MAG SCATTER PISTOL (NC)

Rate of Fire: 2
Accuracy: 3
Shot Power: 4
Effective Range: 1
Ammo Amount: 2
Ammo Type: Shotgun shell (standard)
Damage Type: Direct
Vs. Infantry: 10 x 6 pellets
Vs. Vehicles: 0
Vs. Aircraft: 0
Ammo Type: Shotgun shell (AP)
Damage Type: Direct
Vs. Infantry: 5 x 6 pellets
Vs. Vehicles: 5 x 6 pellets
Vs. Aircraft: 5 x 6 pellets

This magnetically accelerated shotgun pistol fires six pellets that spread rapidly. It deals excellent damage at short or point-blank range. It's next to useless at anything but short range, however.

This gun has a slow rate of fire, but it inflicts considerably more damage per shot than other pistol weapons. It really *is* useless at longer ranges, though, and note that you need to use the right ammo against vehicles and other hard targets; the standard ammo does zero damage to those targets.

This is the weapon of choice for New Conglomerate hackers and scouts in Infiltration Suits; a few quick shots to the back will quickly take down enemies in anything up to Reinforced Exosuits.

NOTE

Damage is listed in terms of pellets. This weapon fires a spread of six pellets, each of which deals a certain amount of damage. For example, if you fire a standard shell at an infantry target and hit with five of the six pellets, your base damage is 50 (10 damage points per pellet that hits).

SUPPRESSOR (COMMON POOL)

Rate of Fire: 3

Accuracy: 4

Shot Power: 2

Effective Range: 3

Ammo Amount: 3

Ammo Type: 9mm standard

Damage Type: Direct

Vs. Infantry: 15

Vs. Vehicles: 8

Vs. Aircraft: 8

Ammo Type: 9mm AP

Damage Type: Direct

Vs. Infantry: 7

Vs. Vehicles: 13

Vs. Aircraft: 13

The Suppressor is the best recourse for the unprepared. If you don't have any advanced weapons Certifications, or you don't have ready access to an Equipment Terminal, this light, general-purpose automatic rifle is absolutely your best bet.

The Suppressor has a 2x zoom, excellent accuracy, and very little recoil, but it suffers from low bullet power. It can equip standard or armor-piercing ammo.

The stats make this gun look worse than certain pistols, but the Suppressor's accuracy and high rate of fire allow you to deal a lot more damage than most pistols at medium to long range. The pistols are better at extremely short range, however.

Also note that if you're fighting vehicles, this weapon is vastly better than the pistols, which in some cases won't even scratch a heavy target.

You can't equip the Suppressor if you're wearing an Infiltration Suit—and always equip a more advanced gun if you have the opportunity. But for times when you just spawned at an AMS that's being attacked, or when you're caught in a battle far from an Equipment Terminal, you can get decent results with the Suppressor.

MEDIUM ASSAULT WEAPONS

Medium assault weapons are both common and effective. While they aren't the pinnacle of weapons technology, they tend to be the best weapons for medium- to long-range fights—especially when you aren't sure what you'll be fighting against.

Other weapons are better than medium assault weapons at specialized, specific tasks, but these general-purpose weapons give you a fighting chance regardless of what you may encounter.

SWEEPER (COMMON POOL)

Rate of Fire: 2

Accuracy: 3

Shot Power: 5

Effective Range: 1

Ammo Amount: 2

Ammo Type: Shotgun shell (standard)

Damage Type: Direct

Vs. Infantry: 10 x 8 pellets

Vs. Vehicles: 5 x 8 pellets

Vs. Aircraft: 5 x 8 pellets

Ammo Type: Shotgun shell (AP)

Damage Type: Direct

Vs. Infantry: 5 x 8 pellets

Vs. Vehicles: 10 x 8 pellets

Vs. Aircraft: 10 x 8 pellets

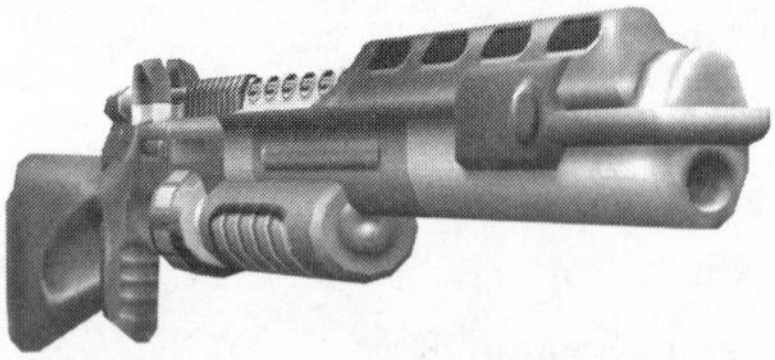

The Sweeper is an extremely powerful short-range weapon. When equipped with the appropriate ammunition it deals excellent damage to any target.

Like the Scatter Pistol, this weapon fires a spread of pellets that widens with distance from the barrel. As a result, it's highly ineffective at medium to long range. It's best indoors against infantry and static targets (like Generators).

It's inadvisable to carry only a Sweeper if you plan to spend any time outdoors, as you'll be helpless at longer ranges. However, the Sweeper is an excellent complement to a longer-range weapon.

PUNISHER (COMMON POOL)

Rate of Fire: 3

Accuracy: 3

Shot Power: 2

Effective Range: 3

Ammo Amount: 3

Ammo Type: 9mm standard

Damage Type: Direct

Vs. Infantry: 18

Vs. Vehicles: 10

Vs. Aircraft: 10

Ammo Type: 9mm AP

Damage Type: Direct

Vs. Infantry: 10

Vs. Vehicles: 15

Vs. Aircraft: 15

Ammo Type: Rocklet

Damage Type: Explosive

Vs. Infantry: 50

Vs. Vehicles: 75

Vs. Aircraft: 75

The Punisher is a twin-barreled weapon. The upper barrel fires a stream of standard or armor-piercing ammo, while the lower barrel fires single rocklets or Fragmentation, Plasma, or Jammer Grenades. It's not a stretch to say this is one of the most versatile weapons in the game.

NOTE

The Punisher can also fire grenade ammunition. See the grenade entries near the end of the chapter for information on each grenade type.

NOTE

Don't pack too much ammo for the lower barrel; it's the upper barrel, and its 9mm ammo, that you'll burn through quickly.

As the lower barrel is single-shot, don't expect to pound an opponent with streams of bullets and grenades simultaneously. However, the added punch of the lower barrel often makes the difference between victory and defeat.

The Punisher is usually no match for the Sweeper at point-blank range, but it's excellent at anything from medium-short to medium-long range, thanks partly to its 4x scope.

PULSAR (VS)

Rate of Fire: 3

Accuracy: 4

Shot Power: 3

Effective Range: 4

Ammo Amount: 3

Ammo Type: Energy cell (primary mode)

Damage Type: Direct

Vs. Infantry: 18

Vs. Vehicles: 10

Vs. Aircraft: 10

Ammo Type: Energy cell (AP mode)

Damage Type: Direct

Vs. Infantry: 10

Vs. Vehicles: 15

Vs. Aircraft: 15

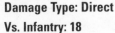

This energy-based rifle is a lot like the Beamer pistol. It uses energy cell ammunition exclusively and can switch between anti-infantry and armor-piercing modes with a tap of the secondary fire button.

The weapon has a built-in 4x zoom, excellent range and accuracy, and low inventory requirements. This makes it a useful general-purpose firearm for any range.

Should you take this weapon or the Punisher? The Pulsar is somewhat more accurate, especially at longer ranges. It's also more inventory-efficient if you face both infantry and hard targets. The Punisher has the advantage of the extra barrel, with its rocklet and grenade ammunition; this gives it a slight edge at closer ranges. You make the call.

CYCLER (TR)

Rate of Fire: 4

Accuracy: 3

Shot Power: 2

Effective Range: 4

Ammo Amount: 4

Ammo Type: 9mm standard

Damage Type: Direct

Vs. Infantry: 18

Vs. Vehicles: 10

Vs. Aircraft: 10

Ammo Type: 9mm AP

Damage Type: Direct

Vs. Infantry: 10

Vs. Vehicles: 15

Vs. Aircraft: 15

The Cycler is the fastest-firing weapon in this class. It can pump out lots of ammo quickly, it has a big magazine (50 bullets), and it's pretty accurate at long range.

This weapon fires faster than the Punisher, so unless you want the versatility of the Punisher's extra ammo types, take this weapon instead. Just be careful to fire in short bursts, as accuracy degrades quickly with constant fire. The Cycler has a 4x zoom.

GAUSS RIFLE (NC)

Rate of Fire: 3

Accuracy: 4

Shot Power: 3

Effective Range: 4

Ammo Amount: 3

Ammo Type: 9mm standard

Damage Type: Direct

Vs. Infantry: 20

Vs. Vehicles: 10

Vs. Aircraft: 10

Ammo Type: 9mm AP

Damage Type: Direct

Vs. Infantry: 12

Vs. Vehicles: 15

Vs. Aircraft: 15

The Gauss Rifle is the New Conglomerate's standard assault rifle, complete with 4x zoom, excellent range, and high accuracy.

This weapon doesn't fire as quickly as the Cycler, but each bullet deals a little more damage vs. infantry targets.

The Gauss Rifle is a little more accurate than the Punisher, and it inflicts a little more damage per shot—so once again, unless you value the Punisher's ammo variety, go with the Gauss Rifle for most tasks.

HEAVY ASSAULT WEAPONS

Each Empire has a single heavy assault weapon. Unlike medium assault weapons, which tend to be very similar, these are all distinctive weapons. To some degree, these weapons parallel their respective Empires' strengths.

LASHER (VS)

Rate of Fire: 3

Accuracy: 3

Shot Power: 4

Effective Range: 2

Ammo Amount: 3

Ammo Type: Energy cell

Damage Type: Standard

Vs. Infantry: 30

Vs. Vehicles: 30

Vs. Aircraft: 30

The Lasher is unlike any other weapon. It fires a relatively slow-moving energy orb that lashes energy tendrils at any targets it passes. A direct hit with the orb deals high damage, but near-misses are also useful, thanks to the lashing effect.

The weapon will not lash at friendly units.

This weapon works best as a room clearer; its ability to damage multiple targets is useful on a crowded battlefield or in close quarters. Its lack of distinction between targets is typical of the Vanu Sovereignty; you can use it against infantry or hard targets without changing ammunition or fire modes (there's only one mode).

This is not a great weapon for long-range combat, so you may want to carry a second weapon or stick to closer-range situations.

NOTE

The lashing ability lets you damage enemies hiding behind cover, and it doesn't require very accurate aim. Learn to use these advantages for a minor edge in hit-and-run fights.

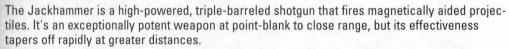

MINI-CHAINGUN (TR)

Rate of Fire: 5
Accuracy: 3
Shot Power: 3
Effective Range: 2
Ammo Amount: 5
Ammo Type: 9mm standard
Damage Type: Direct
Vs. Infantry: 18
Vs. Vehicles: 10
Vs. Aircraft: 10
Ammo Type: 9mm AP
Damage Type: Direct
Vs. Infantry: 10
Vs. Vehicles: 15
Vs. Aircraft: 15

The Mini-Chaingun is a ferocious weapon at close to mid-range. It shoots more bullets in a shorter time frame than any other weapon, and it does so with only moderate bullet spread and recoil. It also has a very large magazine, so you can fire a long time uninterrupted.

A Mini-Chaingun can wreak havoc on both infantry and vehicle targets, due to its exceptional fire rate. Heavy assault weapons tend to be quite specialized as a class, but the Mini-Chaingun is fairly versatile, capable of dealing extreme damage up close or good damage at medium range.

As with the other heavy assault weapons, however, there are limits. This weapon isn't accurate enough to be very effective over long distances.

Overall, the Mini-Chaingun is considered one of the Terran Republic's strongest weapons.

JACKHAMMER (NC)

Rate of Fire: 2
Accuracy: 3
Shot Power: 5
Effective Range: 1
Ammo Amount: 3
Ammo Type: Shotgun shell (standard)
Damage Type: Direct
Vs. Infantry: 10 x 8 pellets
Vs. Vehicles: 5 x 8 pellets
Vs. Aircraft: 5 x 8 pellets
Ammo Type: Shotgun shell (AP)
Damage Type: Direct
Vs. Infantry: 5 x 8 pellets
Vs. Vehicles: 10 x 8 pellets
Vs. Aircraft: 10 x 8 pellets

The Jackhammer is a high-powered, triple-barreled shotgun that fires magnetically aided projectiles. It's an exceptionally potent weapon at point-blank to close range, but its effectiveness tapers off rapidly at greater distances.

The main thing that separates the Jackhammer from the Sweeper, another shotgun-style weapon, is the secondary fire mode. The secondary fire mode unloads all three barrels in rapid succession (faster than you can manually fire in primary mode). This results in spectacular damage if you're close to the target. Despite this mode's raw damage potential, it can't compensate for being too far from the target, and it does force a reload.

This is an exceptionally potent weapon at close range, but choose something else for longer-range work. Also, make the most of the alternate fire mode, as it's this weapon's ace in the hole in a close-quarters duel.

ANTI-VEHICLE WEAPONS

Anti-vehicle weapons have bulky, limited ammunition, slow firing rates, and only moderate anti-personnel capabilities. They make up for all these drawbacks with their ability to punch through heavy armor. Since most weapons are either ineffective or only moderately effective versus vehicles and other hard targets, anti-vehicle weapons are well worth their Certification.

NOTE

The stat rankings for anti-vehicle weapons are separate from those of other weapons. These weapons are unique, so they shouldn't be compared directly with standard weapons.

LANCER (VS)

Rate of Fire: 4

Accuracy: 3

Shot Power: 1

Effective Range: 3

Ammo Amount: 4

Ammo Type: Lancer cartridge

Damage Type: Direct

Vs. Infantry: 50

Vs. Vehicles: 125

Vs. Aircraft: 125

The Lancer is the most unusual anti-vehicle weapon. Instead of a rocket, it fires an energy beam that deals modest damage against infantry but very good damage against MAXes and vehicular targets.

The Lancer takes a half second to fire after the trigger is pulled. Continue tracking your target until the beam is actually discharged.

The Lancer deals less damage per shot than the other anti-vehicle weapons, but it fires much faster. Once you've learned to aim it properly, you'll find that you can deal excellent damage by keeping the crosshairs over your target while unleashing several bolts.

NOTE

It takes time to get good with the Lancer. The aiming takes some getting used to, and you have to remind yourself that you can fire quite rapidly—at least compared with the other anti-vehicle weapons.

STRIKER (TR)

Rate of Fire: 3

Accuracy: 3

Shot Power: 3

Effective Range: 3

Ammo Amount: 3

Ammo Type: Striker missile

Damage Type: Explosive

Vs. Infantry: 50

Vs. Vehicles: 200

Vs. Aircraft: 200

The Striker is a middle-of-the-road anti-vehicle weapon. You aim at the target and wait for a tone to indicate a lock (also, the crosshairs change color). The missile homes in on the target with its secondary fire mode. Keep the crosshairs pointed at the target until the missile strikes; otherwise, it loses guidance and becomes a "dumb-fire" (i.e., straight-flying) missile.

The primary fire mode is a dedicated dumb-fire mode, useful for shooting at static targets or non-vehicle targets.

The Striker uses large missile cartridges. You can shoot missiles several in a row without reloading. The missiles deal middle-of-the-road damage for anti-vehicle weapons.

PHOENIX (NC)

Rate of Fire: 1

Accuracy: 5

Shot Power: 4

Effective Range: 4

Ammo Amount: 1

Ammo Type: Phoenix missile

Damage Type: Explosive

Vs. Infantry: 50

Vs. Vehicles: 300

Vs. Aircraft: 300

The Phoenix is a potent, camera-guided, anti-vehicle missile launcher. As soon as the missile is fired, your perspective shifts to that of the missile, and you can steer it. Press fire again to manually detonate the missile.

The Phoenix loads a single missile at a time, so you must reload between shots. Missiles are bulky, and you can't carry many at once. Also, your character is immobile and helpless while you're flying the missile.

The Phoenix's guidable missile allows you to aim with extreme precision, a useful trait when you're trying to hit agile targets such as Reavers. It also allows you to shoot from a position of cover, attacking targets from afar without exposing yourself to damage. Shooting over walls, for example, is common.

Phoenix missiles fly a long time. You can often adjust course after a near-miss, for example, and loop back for another try at the target. Or you can steer toward a different target altogether.

Overall, the Phoenix's pros vastly outweigh cons. The ability to fire over walls or around trees allows you to make incredible, low-risk shots—and the missile's power is nearly unmatched. Finally, it must be said that flying a missile is a whole lot of fun.

SNIPING WEAPONS

There's only one sniper weapon, and it's the Bolt Driver. It's both potent and very limited; most players either use it a lot or completely avoid it. Only experimentation will tell you which camp you belong to.

BOLT DRIVER (COMMON POOL)

Rate of Fire: 1

Accuracy: 5

Shot Power: 5

Effective Range: 5

Ammo Amount: 1

Ammo Type: Bolt projectile

Damage Type: Direct

Vs. Infantry: 100

Vs. Vehicles: 50

Vs. Aircraft: 50

The Bolt Driver is a single-shot sniper rifle with an 8x zoom. The need to reload after every shot is a drawback, and the bulky bolt ammunition consumes lots of inventory space. However, at extreme range there is nothing that can match its power. It can kill any non-MAX in two shots.

Since the rifle demands extreme accuracy, it's more effective from a crouch. Also, aim at a specific point and let the target run to that point, rather than trying to continuously track the target. This is because moving the weapon increases the cone of fire, and accuracy suffers.

With all these limitations, you might wonder what the value of the weapon is. It's quite useful for large-scale battles, where both attackers and defenders can gain by swiftly picking off infantry, clearing the way for troops attacking the enemy facility (or AMS). It's also great for harassing players at ranges they simply can't return fire from.

SPECIAL ASSAULT WEAPONS

Special assault weapons are a strange bunch. They include the Decimator, which is really an anti-vehicle weapon, and a couple of weapons that are harder to classify. One thing's for sure: Though none of these are mainstay weapons that you'd use in a long-range rifle fight, they're all very potent in specific situations.

DECIMATOR (COMMON POOL)

Rate of Fire: 2

Accuracy: 2

Shot Power: 5

Effective Range: 1

Ammo Amount: 3

Ammo Type: Built-in missiles

Damage Type: Explosive

Vs. Infantry: 50

Vs. Vehicles: 400

Vs. Aircraft: 400

The Decimator is really an anti-vehicle weapon, despite its categorization. It's a three-shot disposable rocket launcher that's extremely potent against armored targets such as MAXes and vehicles, less so against infantry. When all three shots are fired, the Decimator is automatically discarded.

Unlike the Empire-specific anti-vehicle missile launchers, the Decimator is dumb-fire (i.e., unguided). This has pluses and minuses. The plus is that it's easy to fire at non-moving targets and then get out of the way. The minus is that moving targets are harder to hit, and you can't weave through obstacles, up and over walls, and under gates as you would with the other weapons. It's tough to hit distant and fast-moving targets—but when you *do* hit, the damage is unmatched.

The secondary fire mode enables a camera that allows you to see from the missile's perspective (as with the Phoenix), but you can't actually alter the missile's trajectory; it's just for information purposes.

This is the most deadly weapon for destroying hard targets at medium or close range.

ROCKLET RIFLE (COMMON POOL)

Rate of Fire: 2

Accuracy: 3

Shot Power: 3

Effective Range: 3

Ammo Amount: 2

Ammo Type: Rocklet projectile

Damage Type: Explosive

Vs. Infantry: 50

Vs. Vehicles: 75

Vs. Aircraft: 75

The Rocklet Rifle is a strange beast that's fairly good at destroying all target types. It shoots reasonably fast, unguided mini-rockets that are effective to medium-long range.

The secondary fire mode unloads all remaining rocklets in the magazine in rapid succession. The result is excellent damage, but be sure you've got a good shot—you're forced to reload after performing this maneuver.

This is a hard weapon to categorize. It's mainly an anti-vehicle and anti-MAX weapon, but it can be used against infantry in a pinch. Its secondary fire mode makes it much more valuable in close combat than dedicated anti-vehicle weapons, giving it another injection of versatility.

Give the Rocklet Rifle a try; you may prefer it to the dedicated anti-vehicle weapons.

THUMPER (COMMON POOL)

Rate of Fire: 2

Accuracy: 3

Shot Power: 4

Effective Range: 2

Ammo Amount: 2

Ammo Type: Various (see description)

Damage Type: Various

Vs. Infantry: Various

Vs. Vehicles: Various

Vs. Aircraft: Various

The Thumper grenade launcher can fire any type of grenade: Plasma, Fragmentation, or Jammer. Refer to the entries for those grenades for details on their damage and characteristics.

This weapon's slow rate of fire and inability to carry lots of ammo make it a support weapon rather than a standard weapon. A lone soldier running into a firefight probably wouldn't equip this weapon, but a squad member might fire it into a group of enemies, or through a doorway that likely contains enemies. It can hurt opponents behind cover or simply add firepower to a concentrated assault.

It's nice to have one or two Thumpers in every squad, but you wouldn't want everyone to have one. Some squad members should have straight-shooting weapons instead.

MAX WEAPONS

The following section lists stats for MAX weapons. We've provided damage information for the weapons' ammunition but left the generalities for the descriptions. Since there isn't much choice in the matter—your MAX choice is dictated by your Empire—the main thing is just to understand the major differences between the weapon systems.

ANTI-PERSONNEL MAX WEAPONS

Ammo Type: NC Scattercannon

Damage Type: Direct

Vs. Infantry: 10 x 10 pellets

Vs. Vehicles: 5 x 10 pellets

Vs. Aircraft: 5 x 10 pellets

Ammo Type: TR Pounder
Damage Type: Explosive
Vs. Infantry: 70
Vs. Vehicles: 50
Vs. Aircraft: 50

Ammo Type: VS Quasar (normal mode)
Damage Type: Direct
Vs. Infantry: 20
Vs. Vehicles: 10
Vs. Aircraft: 10
Ammo Type: VS Quasar (AP mode)
Damage Type: Direct
Vs. Infantry: 10
Vs. Vehicles: 20
Vs. Aircraft: 20

The various anti-personnel MAXes are all very effective against infantry and moderately effective against hard targets.

The NC Scattercannon is essentially a big shotgun that fires 10-pellet bursts. It features three firing modes, each with a farther zoom, a longer refire delay, and a tighter shot spread. It features plentiful ammo and can be effective out to medium-long range when using the tightest spread.

The Pounder fires mortar-style shells with more of a trajectory than the Falcon's straight-shooting rockets. The damage and fire rate are similar, though, and the damage radius is large.

The Quasar fires laser beams almost as fast as the Dual Cycler spits bullets. Its main advantage is its ability to switch to a secondary armor-piercing fire mode, which gives it a real edge against vehicles (and other MAXes). This makes it extra-versatile, but the downside is that it's not quite as effective against infantry as the other two, and the armor-piercing mode eats double the ammo.

ANTI-VEHICLE MAX WEAPONS

Ammo Type: NC Falcon
Damage Type: Explosive
Vs. Infantry: 35
Vs. Vehicles: 50
Vs. Aircraft: 50

Ammo Type: TR Dual Cycler
Damage Type: Direct
Vs. Infantry: 16
Vs. Vehicles: 18
Vs. Aircraft: 18

Ammo Type: VS Comet
Damage Type: Aggravated
Vs. Infantry: 15
Vs. Vehicles: 40
Vs. Aircraft: 40

The anti-vehicle MAX weapons are fairly similar. They have modest fire speed and modest ammo magazines; they shoot relatively slow-moving dumb-fire projectiles that deal massive damage to vehicles and decent damage to infantry, but hitting infantry can be difficult.

Aircraft are very susceptible to these projectiles *if* you can hit with them. The difficulty lies in targeting fast-moving aircraft with these dumb-fired projectiles.

The Falcon shoots explosive rockets that must travel a short distance before hitting the target; if they hit inside that distance, they deal impact damage but don't explode. The result is less damage overall.

The Dual Cycler deals less damage per shot but fires in a high-speed frenzy. As a result, it is surprisingly useful against vehicles. It doesn't have any zoom-in ability, though, and is only modestly effective at longer ranges. Both its accuracy and fire rate improve when it is spiked (anchored).

The Comet fires explosive plasma spheres in a straight line. As with the other two weapons, hitting infantry can be a bit tricky. The Comet deals less damage initially than the other two weapons, but its aggravated damage adds up quickly.

NOTE

The Pounder is the most versatile of the three weapons, as its trajectory-style attack lets you shell a general area rather than aiming at a specific target. This can be very useful for softening up an enemy stronghold.

ANTI-AIRCRAFT MAX WEAPONS

Ammo Type: NC Sparrow
Damage Type: Explosive
Vs. Infantry: 25
Vs. Vehicles: 50
Vs. Aircraft: 150

Ammo Type: TR Burster
Damage Type: Explosive
Vs. Infantry: 15
Vs. Vehicles: 25
Vs. Aircraft: 50

Ammo Type: VS Starfire
Damage Type: Aggravated
Vs. Infantry: 12
Vs. Vehicles: 20
Vs. Aircraft: 75

These specialized MAX weapons are singularly excellent at bringing down aircraft but mediocre at everything else.

The Sparrow can fire just a few missiles before needing to be reloaded, but each missile deals excellent damage to aircraft. The missiles can lock onto aircraft and will home in when fired with a lock, but they must be dumb-fired against everything else. Damage against land vehicles is modest, and infantry damage is quite weak.

The Burster fires explosive shells that detonate in the proximity of aircraft. When fired at land targets the shells deal only impact damage. Each shell inflicts substantially less damage than a Sparrow missile, but many more can be fired.

Finally, the Starfire shoots plasma spheres that lock onto air targets and explode for aggravated damage—but as with the other weapons, the plasma will neither lock nor explode when fired at land targets. Its magazine holds slightly more ammunition than the Sparrow's magazine.

GRENADES, ENGINEER EXPLOSIVES, AND TURRETS

The following section covers miscellaneous weapons, including grenades (which anyone can use), explosives created from an ACE device, and two different kinds of turrets. It's useful to compare these stats with those of more traditional weapons.

GRENADES (COMMON POOL)

Ammo Type: Frag Grenade
Damage Type: Explosive
Vs. Infantry: 75
Vs. Vehicles: 100
Vs. Aircraft: 100

Ammo Type: Plasma Grenade
Damage Type: Aggravated
Vs. Infantry: 40
Vs. Vehicles: 30
Vs. Aircraft: 30

Ammo Type: Jammer Grenade
Damage Type: —
Vs. Infantry: —
Vs. Vehicles: —
Vs. Aircraft: —

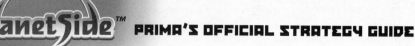

Grenades can be lobbed by hand and grenade ammo packs can be shot from a Thumper or Punisher. Switch the fire mode to change from "explode on contact" to a three-second fuse.

Fragmentation Grenades are excellent against both infantry and hard targets, while Plasma Grenades are best against infantry. Jammer Grenades do no damage, but they:

- Detonate any HE Mines or Boomers in the area.
- Temporarily deactivate any Spitfire Turrets and Motion Sensors.
- Temporarily deactivate players' Implants.

As you can see, Jammer Grenades are useful for a wide variety of tasks. Toss them into hostile territory before charging in, and you may save yourself some headaches.

Use grenades' three-second mode for throwing around corners; select the "explode on contact" mode for direct assaults.

When throwing grenades by hand, hold the button down longer for longer throws.

ENGINEERS' EXPLOSIVES (COMMON POOL)

HE MINES

Ammo Type: ACE
Damage Type: Explosive
Vs. Infantry: 100
Vs. Vehicles: 500
Vs. Aircraft: 500

HE Mines deal enough damage to kill an unarmored or previously injured character outright. They also deal massive damage to any vehicle unfortunate enough to drive over them.

The anti-vehicle aspect of HE Mines is underutilized by most players. Look for likely vehicle spots and throw down a few of these mines; you may be surprised at the damage they inflict.

BOOMERS

Ammo Type: ACE
Damage Type: Explosive
Vs. Infantry: 250
Vs. Vehicles: 400
Vs. Aircraft: 400

Boomers are remote-controlled explosives that deal slightly less damage to vehicles than HE Mines. They're damaging enough to kill infantry in *any* non-MAX armor outright, if you score a direct hit.

TURRETS (COMMON POOL)

SPITFIRE TURRET

Ammo Type: ACE

Damage Type: Direct

Vs. Infantry: 15

Vs. Vehicles: 10

Vs. Aircraft: 10

Spitfire Turrets fire a stream of lead comparable to that of most good assault rifles. Walk past them to avoid them, or destroy them from a position of safety.

SUMMARY

PlanetSide weapons have many differences, some subtle, some not so subtle. Many situations call for a general type of weapon, and it's not that important which one you choose; it's just important that you understand that weapon's quirks and limitations, and know how to use it.

Even more importantly, you need to avoid weapons that are inappropriate for the task at hand. Getting into a long-range firefight with a Sweeper is ludicrous, as is charging a pack of infantry in a Starfire MAX. If you pick a weapon that's more or less right for the job, you don't need to worry about whether your opponent's weapon is fractionally better. Skill, tactics, and superior numbers will win the day nine times out of 10.

This chapter has given you the tools you need to understand *PlanetSide*'s weapons. Learn them all, and understand their uses. When you instinctively know what weapon to use for any given situation, you're a big step closer to mastering the game.

CHAPTER 3: ARMOR

Weapons are important, but armor plays an even bigger role in defining what your character can do. Combined with the right Certifications and gear, armor transforms you into a fighting machine, a medic, an engineer, a stealthy assassin, or any combination or variant.

Just as importantly, certain armor types prohibit specific roles or tasks, so when picking armor, keep an eye not only on what you want to do, but on what you *won't* be able to do. This is important stuff, so we encourage you to dig deep into the chapter and absorb as much as you can.

ARMOR IN FOCUS

In *PlanetSide*, the type of armor you wear has a big effect on what you can do. You've probably run into this concept in other games, but here, it's taken to the next level. In other games, the tradeoff is typically quite simple: speed vs. armor. Do you want to be fast? Then take the light armor, but beware of getting shot, because you're very fragile. Do you want to be burly and well-protected? Then take the heavy armor, but don't expect to zip around the map.

There are several armor types; each determines not only your speed and amount of armor, but also what you can carry. Armor dictates both inventory *size* (the total amount of stuff you can lug around) and inventory *shape* (the size and shape of individual weapons or tools that you can use). Furthermore, certain armor types provide unique powers (such as cloaking or super jumps) and restrictions (such as limiting your turning speed).

The next few pages examine each armor type in detail, pointing out strengths and weaknesses, as well as suitability for various roles.

NOTE

As with weapon stats, armor stats may be tweaked during PlanetSide's existence. Because of this, the numbers here are abstractions; they will likely change, but they're also likely to stay in proportion to each other. In other words, use the numbers to get a general sense of what each armor type is capable of, but don't try to do calculations with them.

EXPLANATION OF VALUES

Total Armor is simply the total amount of protection. Whenever the armor absorbs damage, this value decreases. **Walk Speed** and **Run Speed** are self-explanatory. They're presented in meters per second.

NOTE

Having a weapon or tool in your hands affects your speed! Players in every armor type (except for MAXes) run 1.5 meters per second *slower* with an equipped item in hand. So put away those guns when you want to run quickly.

Threshold is the amount of damage the armor reduces per attack. **Direct Threshold** reduces damage from direct hits by projectiles, **Explosive Threshold** reduces damage from explosive weapons and splash damage, and **Aggravated Threshold** reduces damage from weapons that deal aggravated (burn) damage.

For example, let's say a Standard Exosuit is hit by a bullet that normally does 10 points of damage. The Standard Exosuit has a Direct Threshold of 4, so it blocks 4 points; therefore, only 6 points get through to damage the character's health. The Total Armor value is also reduced by 4, to reflect the damage that the armor absorbed. When the Total Armor value gets near zero, you effectively have no more protection.

Pistol Slots and **Rifle Slots** are the number of "holsters" your character has for weapons and gear. Pistol slots can accommodate pistol-sized weapons and tools, and rifle slots are for rifle-sized weapons and tools).

Inventory Space is the total size of the armor's general inventory. It's expressed as a number of squares, like 6x9 or 12x12.

NOTE

For your reference: A pistol-sized weapon takes up 3x3 inventory squares. A rifle takes up 9x3 inventory squares.

Finally, **Base BEP Value** is the base number of BEPs an opponent will collect by killing you while you're wearing this armor. Several modifiers apply, though; refer to chapter 7 for more about the BEP system.

STANDARD EXOSUIT

Total Armor: 50
Walk Speed: 3
Run Speed: 6
Direct Threshold: 4
Explosive Threshold: 15
Aggravated Threshold: 8
Pistol Slots: 1
Rifle Slots: 1
Inventory Space: 6x9
Base BEP Value: 100

Oh, my. You aren't going to run around in *that*, are you?

Well, you probably will—at least when you first appear in the game, and whenever you respawn. A Standard Exosuit is the default armor for new characters, and until you find a friendly Equipment Terminal, it's all you've got.

The Standard Exosuit's main virtues are that it's quite fast, and it doesn't prevent you from driving any vehicles or mounting any turrets. Its disadvantages are more numerous.

Standard Exosuits provide very little protection; only the Infiltration Suit is less protective. Your inventory is limited. You can equip one rifle-sized item and one pistol-sized item, and carry a modest load of extra gear.

Why, you may ask, would one choose to wear this armor? And why does it exist in the first place?

The answers are that you generally wouldn't choose it, and that it exists mainly to emphasize the value of Equipment Terminals. If you always started out with great armor, there would be less reason to protect your vital AMS, or to hack an enemy's Inventory Terminal. In short, there would be less incentive to play smart.

Theoretically, you might prefer this armor to an Agile Exosuit because of its fractional speed advantage, but in practice, the Agile Exosuit's superior protection and inventory space provide more than enough reason to immediately make the switch.

AGILE EXOSUIT

Total Armor: 100

Walk Speed: 3

Run Speed: 5.5

Direct Threshold: 6

Explosive Threshold: 25

Aggravated Threshold: 10

Pistol Slots: 2

Rifle Slots: 1

Inventory Space: 9x9

Base BEP Value: 125

From the name, you might expect an Agile Exosuit to be faster but less protective than a Standard Exosuit. It's actually the other way around; Agile Exosuits are fractionally slower, but substantially more protective, than Standard Exosuits. They also have considerably more inventory space. Everyone starts with Agile Exosuit Certification.

Agile Exosuits are not suitable for heavy combat roles, and they're not sneaky like Infiltration Suits. So what good are they?

They're useful for players who want to snipe or engage in hit-and-run tactics with a rifle-sized weapon, as well as for drivers who spend most of their time in vehicles and don't want to spend extra Certification Points on Infiltration Suits. And they're useful for anyone who prefers a nimble though fragile fighter to a heavy, durable one.

NOTE

Players in Agile Exosuits can pilot any vehicle, occupy any turret or gunner position, and ride in any vehicle's passenger position that isn't specifically set aside for MAXes.

Since Agile Exosuits are better in most ways than the Standard Exosuit, and since they don't disqualify you from driving vehicles or manning turrets, switch into an Agile Exosuit whenever there's a choice between it and a Standard Exosuit.

Whether you stick with the Agile Exosuit over time depends on your preferred role and style of combat. If you want to be a heavy fighter, move on to Reinforced Battle Armor. But even then, it's handy to have the Agile Exosuit as a backup for piloting a vehicle, manning a turret, or sniping.

REINFORCED BATTLE ARMOR

Total Armor: 150

Walk Speed: 3

Run Speed: 4.5

Direct Threshold: 8

Explosive Threshold: 35

Aggravated Threshold: 12

Pistol Slots: 2

Rifle Slots: 2

Inventory Space: 9x12

Base BEP Value: 150

Reinforced Battle Armor (sometimes called the Reinforced Exosuit) provides a number of distinct advantages, though it's not without its drawbacks. It's the armor of choice for players who want to fight effectively but also have the versatility to play other roles.

Reinforced Battle Armor's strengths include very good protection, excellent inventory space, and multiple holsters that allow you to have many weapons and tools at the ready. Its wearers can also pilot some vehicles, though restrictions apply.

NOTE

Characters in Reinforced Battle Armor can pilot any vehicle with an open cockpit. These include the Assault Basilisk, Wraith, Harasser, and the various Assault Buggies. Closed cockpit vehicles cannot be piloted.

Wearers of Reinforced Battle Armor can be passengers or gunners in any vehicle but cannot occupy passenger slots reserved for MAXes.

This armor's primary disadvantage is speed; Reinforced Battle Armor is the slowest armor type. MAXes are also slow, but their special run mode allows them to get from one place to another quickly, at the expense of their offense. Reinforced Battle Armor lacks that mode, and players in it can't pilot every vehicle—so it's important to have open-cockpit vehicles (or friendly drivers) nearby.

Reinforced Battle Armor is an excellent choice for medics, engineers, and any character who needs to carry specialized gear in addition to weaponry. It's also great for players who enjoy front-line combat. Some players may prefer the agility of Agile Exosuits, but *PlanetSide*'s cone-of-fire system (see chapter 8) makes running and gunning less viable than in other action games and emphasizes the protective value of Reinforced Battle Armor.

INFILTRATION SUIT

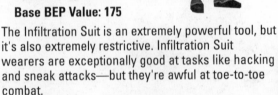

Total Armor: 0

Walk Speed: 3

Run Speed: 6.5

Direct Threshold: 0

Explosive Threshold: 0

Aggravated Threshold: 0

Pistol Slots: 1

Rifle Slots: 0

Inventory Space: 6x6

Base BEP Value: 175

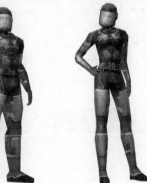

The Infiltration Suit is an extremely powerful tool, but it's also extremely restrictive. Infiltration Suit wearers are exceptionally good at tasks like hacking and sneak attacks—but they're awful at toe-to-toe combat.

NOTE

Those wearing Infiltration Suits can pilot any vehicle, occupy any turret or gunner position, and ride in any vehicle's passenger position that isn't specifically set aside for MAXes.

Infiltration Suits provide zero actual protection, so wearers are absolutely dependent on stealth. They can only wield pistol-sized weapons, and inventory is extremely limited.

The Infiltration Suit's one big advantage is its cloak. When activated, the cloak makes the wearer mostly invisible. Standing still results in true invisibility, while movement renders the wearer slightly visible. Running or firing exposes the wearer.

Players with Darklight Vision can see players in Infiltration Suits. But since Darklight Vision drains Stamina, it cannot be used all the time. Also, its visual range is poor, so it's not a cure-all against stealthy intruders.

Infiltration Suited players can equip a pistol or use a knife; emptying a full pistol clip in someone's back will result in a kill, except when dealing with MAXes. Players in this armor can also carry ACE devices, which allows them to be stealthy engineers.

The bottom line is that Infiltration Suits are excellent for stealthy hacking, assassination, and deployment of ACE devices. They're also great for characters who drive vehicles or operate turrets, because they allow you to be unseen during the vulnerable times when you're not in a turret or vehicle. They're completely unsuitable for outright combat, though, and they're fragile enough that being seen usually results in swift death.

Infiltration Suits can change the way you play the game. We strongly recommend trying them, if only to learn their advantages and disadvantages firsthand.

MAX ARMOR

Total Armor: 650

Walk Speed: 3.75

Run Speed: 12

Direct Threshold: —

Explosive Threshold: —

Aggravated Threshold: —

Pistol Slots: —

Rifle Slots: —

Inventory Space: 16x12

Base BEP Value: 250

A MAX is a hulking suit of powered armor with some characteristics of a vehicle. It is massive and distinctive; you'll learn to distinguish a MAX from a regular soldier very quickly.

All MAXes feature a built-in arm weapon. This weapon is extremely powerful. Couple this with the MAX's extraordinary armor, and you have a deadly unit.

Each faction has three MAX variants: an anti-personnel MAX, an anti-air MAX, and an anti-vehicle MAX. The difference lies entirely in the built-in arm weapon; the anti-air MAX's weapon is excellent at destroying aerial vehicles, for example, but not as effective against land vehicles or infantry.

A MAX moves slower than a character in any other armor type, *unless* you press the Autorun key (default 🔘). Whereas Autorun is merely a convenience in other armor types, allowing you to check the map or swap guns as you cross the map, it engages a completely different system for a MAX. A MAX with Autorun engaged cannot fire its weapons; it can only run. It starts out slowly but gradually builds speed. Eventually, an Autorunning MAX attains about twice the speed of a running player in an Agile Exosuit.

On the down side, a running MAX takes corners slowly, so precise, hairpin turns are out of the question. Also, it takes a while to slow down from top speed, and you cannot fire until the MAX has fully slowed to a walk.

MAXes have limited rotation and gun-aiming speed. Think of it as a weapon turret on a heavy vehicle; you simply can't turn it very fast.

As a result of this restriction, aiming with a MAX takes some getting used to. Also, fast targets at close range can cause problems for a MAX, as they can sometimes elude its gun.

GENERAL MAX CHARACTERISTICS

Despite their ability to mow down legions of foes, MAXes are still very limited. They're great in confrontations with individuals or small groups of their designated enemy type (infantry for the anti-personnel MAX, for example), but they need help from their friends.

Their inability to use alternative weapons or tools is their biggest weakness. Consider:

- A MAX can only fight. It cannot heal others, repair items, deploy engineer devices, hack into anything, or pilot a vehicle.

- A MAX can heal itself with Medkits, but it cannot repair its own armor—and armor is most of its protection. Therefore, it needs friendly players to repair its armor.

- With only one weapon (albeit a very powerful weapon), a MAX can't adjust to every situation. For example, an anti-vehicle MAX can't switch to an anti-personnel weapon when infantry attack, and an anti-infantry MAX that's being sniped can't pull out its own sniper rifle.

- MAXes excel at fighting but have a hard time with enemies that use terrain to hide, or enemies that sneak away. This is caused by slow foot speed and limited turning radius.

- MAXes will never surprise you, because their range of tactics and activities is so limited. A creative opponent will actively try to pick on the MAX's weaknesses, or simply avoid the MAX and get on with whatever he or she was doing before.

- MAX armor cannot be purchased at an AMS. It's only available at full-sized Equipment Terminals.

- As with vehicles, MAX armor has a purchase delay of several minutes. If you're destroyed immediately and then try to get another MAX of the same type, you're locked out and must wait until the timer expires.

A few more things to consider:

MAX armor works differently than other armor types. Instead of having a Threshold, it simply absorbs *all* damage from all sources. It does this until the Total Armor value is reduced to zero, at which time the MAX wearer will take damage.

MAXes cannot pilot any vehicle or occupy any turret or gunner's position. They can be passengers only on vehicles with designated MAX passenger slots: specifically, the Sunderer and the Galaxy.

Though they can't use standard weapons or tools, MAXes can carry lots of ammunition and Medkits thanks to their excellent inventory capacity. In a well-organized squad, they can also carry ammo or extra gear for other squad members, dropping or trading the gear whenever necessary.

FACTION VARIATIONS

Each faction's MAX uses a unique weapons system. Refer to chapter 2 for details on MAX weapons. Each faction's MAX has a special ability that draws on a built-in power source, which slowly replenishes when the power is not being used.

New Conglomerate MAXes can engage a shield, which absorbs damage in combat and makes them extra-tough. The shield drops when the MAX fires, but it's very useful for charging into position (or retreating).

Terran Republic MAXes have the "spike" ability; they can anchor to the ground and fire faster, suffering less recoil. The downside is immobility; they have to "unspike" before they can go anywhere.

Vanu Sovereignty MAXes can jump great distances. For example, a Vanu Sovereignty MAX can leap from an installation courtyard up to a second-floor walkway. Press and hold the Jump key (default space) for higher jumps.

SPECIFIC MAX TYPES

Chapter 2 contains the hard data for MAX weapons, but here's an overview of the three MAX types' different weapons.

ANTI-PERSONNEL MAX

Anti-personnel MAXes are the most common type. Most enemies are on foot, so anti-personnel MAXes have a wide choice of targets.

Anti-personnel MAXes are great defenders. They can patrol a friendly base, wiping out intruders in the courtyard area or lurking inside to crush would-be hackers.

Anti-personnel MAXes are also vital to base-capturing efforts. If the enemy has MAXes inside—and they very probably do—it's important to bring your own MAXes to clean them out. Without them, your invasion force is likely to suffer a quick and painful demise.

ANTI-VEHICLE MAX

Anti-vehicle MAXes are great at taking down Wall Turrets, vehicles, and other MAXes. They fire shell-type weapons that are very deadly to heavily armored targets. Their slow rate of fire makes them more vulnerable to infantry attacks, though they can still be effective against infantry.

Thanks to their effectiveness against other MAXes, anti-vehicle MAXes are useful both inside and out.

ANTI-AIR MAX

Anti-air MAXes are the most specialized MAX, which is why their Certification costs less. They fire projectiles that lock onto aerial targets and home in on them, dealing excellent damage. Ground targets can be destroyed as well, but the projectiles won't lock on, and in some cases they deal reduced damage.

Needless to say, anti-air MAXes are best outdoors.

FINAL ANALYSIS

It's a cliché to say that every armor has its own strengths and weaknesses, and that you should choose your armor based on what tasks you want to accomplish. However, in this case the cliché is absolutely true. There are no useless armor types in *PlanetSide*; only the Standard Exosuit is appreciably weaker than the others, and that's for a good reason (to emphasize the value of Equipment Terminals). All the others have legitimate strengths and weaknesses, and choosing an armor type really *is* a matter of figuring out what sort of role you want to play.

Experiment with them all; you'll eventually discover your favorites. Even if you decide you hate a particular armor type, it's very instructive to play it awhile. This lets you discover its strengths and weaknesses firsthand and gives you an edge when fighting that armor type in future battles.

CHAPTER 4: VEHICLES

Vehicles are more useful in *PlanetSide* than in other combat games you may have played. This is partly due to the sheer size of the game world; running across an entire continent, or even a quarter of a continent, is not a practical method of travel.

There are other reasons. Certain vehicles, such as the AMS and ANT, are absolutely critical to maintaining a working Empire. Without them, most assaults would be impractical, and your bases would soon run out of power. Also, the sheer logistical difficulty of getting large groups from one spot to another makes transport vehicles very attractive.

Finally, there's no denying the impact a powerful combat vehicle can have, whether you're patrolling a friendly base, breaking apart an enemy AMS, or guarding a Deliverer or Sunderer packed with friendly troops.

This chapter provides stats for every vehicle, a detailed look at vehicles' strengths and weaknesses, and their suitability for various roles. By the time you're done here you'll know how to use every vehicle in the game.

VEHICLE STATS AND CHARACTERISTICS

Vehicles are rated in the following categories:

Top Speed: Expressed in KPH

Acceleration: An abstract value from 1 to 5, 5 being the best

Maneuverability: An abstract value from 1 to 5, 5 being the best

Total Armor: Starting armor points of the vehicle

Threshold: Amount of damage subtracted from any attack on the vehicle

Gunners: Number of gunner spots on the vehicle

Passengers: Number of non-gunner passenger spots on the vehicle

Weapons: Description of the vehicle's weapons

Threshold is the one stat that demands extra explanation. Some vehicles are very durable, and Threshold represents that durability. Every time an attack hits the vehicle, the Threshold value is subtracted from the attack, and any remaining damage points are applied to the armor. For example, an attack dealing 15 points of damage hits an AMS, which has a Threshold of 10. The Threshold value is subtracted from the attack, leaving only 5 points of damage, which are subtracted from the Total Armor.

NOTE

When vehicles reach 10 percent or less of their total armor, you lose control of them. This is your clue that it's time to bail out. If you stay inside the vehicle any longer, it explodes and your character will die.

Vehicles that have weapons have stats for those weapons. The weapon stats are expressed as follows:

Weapon Type: Name of weapon

Damage Type: Type of damage (direct, explosive, aggravated). This is important because some types of armor are better against certain types of attack.

Vs. Infantry: Damage per shot the weapon deals to infantry

Vs. Vehicles: Damage per shot the weapon deals to vehicles

Vs. Aircraft: Damage per shot the weapon deals to aircraft

NOTE

Weapons with the same name can perform differently on different vehicles. The stats are always the bottom line.

A few other notes about vehicles:

Land vehicles are very hard to flip over. If you do upend them, however, they become useless; time to look for another one. The same applies when you drive a vehicle into deep water!

A vehicle that hits a soldier at less than 30 percent throttle pushes that soldier aside, dealing no damage; at 100 percent throttle, the soldier is typically killed. Intermediate throttle values inflict different levels of damage.

The Basilisk, Wraith, Mosquito, and Reaver take just as much damage from colliding with infantry as the infantry takes in return. Assault buggies and the Harasser take only 50 percent damage from such collisions, and heavier vehicles such as tanks and personnel transports take no damage at all.

Thus, while you *can* run over infantry with light vehicles, you'll take collateral damage from it. Be especially careful of MAXes, which are very heavy and deal extra damage in vehicle collisions.

UTILITY VEHICLES

PlanetSide's utility vehicles include the AMS (Advanced Mobile Station) and ANT (Advanced Nanite Transport). Both vehicles are critical to the game.

AMS (ADVANCED MOBILE STATION)

Top Speed: 70

Acceleration: 1

Maneuverability: 1

Total Armor: 3,000

Threshold: 10

Gunners: —

Passengers: —

Weapons: —

The AMS is the key to many assaults. It's a single-seat vehicle with fairly low speed and no weapons, but its functionality becomes apparent when the vehicle is deployed.

A deployed AMS provides a Respawn Tube, a Matrix Panel that players can bind to, and an Equipment Terminal. It also generates a cloaking field that renders it invisible to enemies at a distance; only those who get very close can detect its presence.

Essentially, an AMS is a one-stop launching point for an attack. With an AMS in the vicinity, fallen characters can respawn and re-equip very close to the place they were fighting, then jump right back into the fray. Often this is the key to a successful attack. Similarly, the lack of an AMS causes players to respawn at more distant spots, and this can derail an attack faster than anything.

It's useful to have an AMS on defense, as well. This way, if the base is overrun and its respawn facilities are taken down, defenders can still reappear and re-equip nearby.

AMSes are terribly clumsy and accelerate poorly, but they have a semi-respectable top speed, and their high Threshold and Total Armor values make them just as immune to small weapons as a heavy tank. Don't bother attacking an AMS with pistols—or even rifles, unless you're using armor-piercing ammo.

There's more information on using AMSes in chapters 9 and 11.

ANT (ADVANCED NANITE TRANSPORT)

Top Speed: 45

Acceleration: 1

Maneuverability: 3

Total Armor: 750

Threshold: 5

Gunners: —

Passengers: —

Weapons: —

The ANT is an extremely slow, one-person vehicle used to resupply facilities' power. This is a critical function; if a friendly facility runs completely out of power, your Empire loses control and the facility becomes neutral.

There is no ANT Certification. Possessing a Certification for any other vehicle allows you to purchase and drive an ANT.

The process for resupplying a facility is:

1. Purchase an ANT and drive it to a friendly Warp Gate.
2. Stop near the Warp Gate, get out, and deploy the vehicle.
3. The vehicle starts collecting NTUs (Nanite Technology Units, a.k.a. energy) from the Warp Gate.
4. When the ANT is full of energy, it automatically un-deploys.
5. Drive the ANT to a facility. Get right up next to the NTU silo in the courtyard.
6. Deploy the ANT. It slowly fills the facility up with NTUs, until it's back at 100 percent.

ANTs can fit in the cargo bay of a Galaxy. This is the most efficient way of transporting them, thanks to their atrociously slow top speed.

FOUR-WHEELED CYCLES

While *PlanetSide* is a team game, there are definitely times when you want to travel alone—and when you really want to get from one place to another fast. These four-wheelers allow you to do just that.

ASSAULT BASILISK

Top Speed: 90

Acceleration: 5

Maneuverability: 5

Total Armor: 350

Threshold: 0

Gunners: —

Passengers: —

Weapons: 2 20mm Chainguns

Weapon Type: 20mm Chaingun

Damage Type: Direct

Vs. Infantry: 20

Vs. Vehicles: 20

Vs. Aircraft: 40

The Assault Basilisk is a favorite of lightly armored hackers, scouts, and anyone who wants to get quickly from one spot to another. It's very light and has a pair of forward-mounted chainguns.

It's a fragile vehicle with less armor than a MAX, but its acceleration and maneuverability are excellent. The forward-firing 20mm Chainguns are the real surprise; they deal excellent damage to infantry and are particularly effective against aircraft—*if* you can line them up in your sights. Make no mistake: A skilled driver can get a great deal of combat value out of this small machine.

WRAITH

Top Speed: 90

Acceleration: 5

Maneuverability: 5

Total Armor: 250

Threshold: 0

Gunners: —

Passengers: —

Weapons: —

The Wraith is effectively just a Basilisk with even lighter armor and no guns, unless the driver is wearing an Infiltration Suit. If so, the Wraith becomes cloaked—just like the driver. The result is the ideal transport for spies, scouts, stealth hackers—anyone who plays in an Infiltration Suit. A Wraith on the move can be seen, but at a distance it's usually overlooked.

With one of these vehicles, it's easy to cover a whole lot of ground quickly and stealthily. It's ideal for hunting enemy AMSes and parked Galaxies; you can search a large area very quickly, without the bother of anyone seeing you. And if someone does see you, you can usually just drive away.

ASSAULT BUGGIES

Assault buggies fill the middle ground between four-wheelers and tanks. They tend to be fast, maneuverable, and also fairly durable. They usually shouldn't take on tanks, but they're great against infantry.

HARASSER

Top Speed: 80

Acceleration: 4

Maneuverability: 4

Total Armor: 600

Threshold: 0

Gunners: 1

Passengers: —

Weapons: 12mm Chaingun

Weapon Type: 12mm Chaingun

Damage Type: Direct

Vs. Infantry: 25

Vs. Vehicles: 10

Vs. Aircraft: 25

This basic two-man scout vehicle holds a driver and a gunner, who mans the 12mm Chaingun turret. Think of it as a slightly heavier, slightly better-armored (and slightly slower) Basilisk that can take another passenger.

Compared with the Basilisk, the Harasser has a little less speed and maneuverability, as well as less anti-air power. On the other hand, you get to take a gunner, who has a bigger field of fire with the turret than you'd get from the Basilisk's driver-operated chainguns. Since the gunner doesn't have to worry about driving, you're more likely to be accurate with this vehicle's weapons.

The Harasser is lighter, faster, and much lighter-armed than the Empire-specific buggies we look at next.

MARAUDER (TR)

Top Speed: 80

Acceleration: 3

Maneuverability: 4

Total Armor: 900

Threshold: 5

Gunners: 2

Passengers: —

Weapons: Pounder, 12mm Chaingun

Weapon Type: Pounder

Damage Type: Explosive

Vs. Infantry: 150

Vs. Vehicles: 200

Vs. Aircraft: 200

Weapon Type: 12mm Chaingun

Damage Type: Direct

Vs. Infantry: 25

Vs. Vehicles: 10

Vs. Aircraft: 25

The Marauder is a three-person assault buggy. It holds a driver, a 12mm Chaingun for the side passenger, and a Heavy Grenade Launcher in the rear turret.

The chaingun is good against infantry and air vehicles but weak against other vehicles. The Heavy Grenade Launcher deals serious splash damage and is effective against everything; it tears up infantry and deals vehicle damage equivalent to a heavy tank's main gun!

The keys with this vehicle are to master the aim on the Heavy Grenade Launcher and to keep moving. While the Marauder packs a punch similar to that of a heavy tank, and it's a lot more durable than a Harasser, it's still fragile compared to a tank.

You can view the two gunner slots as either an opportunity or a drawback, depending on how many people you like to travel with.

ENFORCER (NC)

Top Speed: 80

Acceleration: 3

Maneuverability: 4

Total Armor: 1,200

Threshold: 5

Gunners: 1

Passengers: —

Weapons: Firebird Missle System

Weapon Type: Advanced Rocket Launcher

Damage Type: Explosive

Vs. Infantry: 150

Vs. Vehicles: 200

Vs. Aircraft: 200

This well-armored assault buggy sports a Firebird Advanced Rocket Launcher in the rear turret. This weapon packs excellent punch, equivalent to that of a tank.

The Enforcer has slightly less overall firepower than the Marauder, as it lacks the second gunner. Also, its rockets deal a bit less splash damage than the Marauder's grenades. However, the Enforcer is more heavily armored, plus its rockets are easier to aim at most targets than the grenades.

THRESHER (VS)

Top Speed: 70

Acceleration: 3

Maneuverability: 4

Total Armor: 900

Threshold: 5

Gunners: 1

Passengers: —

Weapons: Flux Cannon

Weapon Type: Flux Cannon

Damage Type: Direct

Vs. Infantry: 20

Vs. Vehicles: 40

Vs. Aircraft: 40

The Thresher is a hovercraft-style assault buggy. It has a Flux Cannon mounted in the passenger position; this rapid-fire weapon can take out infantry and vehicles with equal facility.

As a hovercraft, the Thresher can cross water for short periods. Top speed is decreased during this time—and if you run out of air jet power, you'll sink. Be careful!

Threshers and other hover vehicles are more maneuverable than other vehicles; they can strafe as well as drive forward and backward.

The Thresher has somewhat less raw damage output than the other two Empires' assault buggies, but more maneuverability, and a nice trick in its ability to cross water.

TANKS

Tanks are bigger and slower than assault buggies, but their much-increased armor and firepower make them highly effective for combat duty. Their high Threshold values make them practically immune to certain weapons, forcing opponents to attack with anti-vehicle weaponry or get out of the way.

LIGHTNING

Top Speed: 75

Acceleration: 5

Maneuverability: 4

Total Armor: 750

Threshold: 7

Gunners: —

Passengers: —

Weapons: 75mm Cannon, 20mm Chaingun

Weapon Type: 75mm Cannon

Damage Type: Explosive

Vs. Infantry: 75

Vs. Vehicles: 125

Vs. Aircraft: 125

Weapon Type: 20mm Chaingun

Damage Type: Direct

Vs. Infantry: 20

Vs. Vehicles: 20

Vs. Aircraft: 40

Okay, so you can forget what we just said about tanks. The Lightning is a lot more like a one-person assault buggy than a tank, featuring excellent speed, light armor, a 20mm Chaingun, and a 75mm Cannon.

The anti-vehicle cannon doesn't inflict as much damage as some heavy buggy weapons, but it's fast-firing and easy to aim. It also deals some splash damage. The 20mm Chaingun is a good alternative for anti-infantry attacks.

Always remember that the Lightning is not a heavy tank; it's got good weaponry and excellent speed, but despite its good Threshold it's somewhat fragile. You can't plow deep into enemy forces and expect to come out unscathed. Use this vehicle for hit-and-run style attacks instead.

PROWLER (TR)

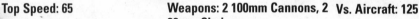

Top Speed: 65

Acceleration: 3

Maneuverability: 3

Total Armor: 2,500

Threshold: 10

Gunners: 2

Passengers: —

Weapons: 2 100mm Cannons, 2 20mm Chainguns

Weapon Type: 100mm Cannon

Damage Type: Explosive

Vs. Infantry: 75

Vs. Vehicles: 125

Vs. Aircraft: 125

Weapon Type: 20mm Chaingun

Damage Type: Direct

Vs. Infantry: 20

Vs. Vehicles: 20

Vs. Aircraft: 40

The Prowler heavy tank seats three, including a driver, a gunner with two 100mm Cannons for destroying heavy targets, and a second gunner with a pair of 20mm Rotary Chainguns.

The cannons fire sequentially, not in tandem. This means you won't deal all your damage in a single punch, but it also means you'll also have a good rate of fire as the two cannons alternate. Over time, the firepower of these two cannons is identical to that of the Vanguard tank's single 150mm Cannon.

The Prowler requires one more gunner than the other two heavy tanks. This can be a pain, but with two independent gunners, it's possible to fire the cannons and chainguns simultaneously, either at the same target or different targets. The Vanguard's lone gunner, on the other hand, must choose between cannon and guns, and can only deal with a single target.

VANGUARD (NC)

Top Speed: 65

Acceleration: 3

Maneuverability: 3

Total Armor: 2,500

Threshold: 10

Gunners: 1

Passengers: —

Weapons: 150mm Cannon, 2 20mm Chainguns

Weapon Type: 150mm Cannon

Damage Type: Explosive

Vs. Infantry: 150

Vs. Vehicles: 250

Vs. Aircraft: 250

Weapon Type: 20mm Chaingun

Damage Type: Direct

Vs. Infantry: 20

Vs. Vehicles: 20

Vs. Aircraft: 40

This heavy New Conglomerate tank features heavy armor, good speed, a 20mm Chaingun, and a 150mm Cannon. Between the chaingun and cannon, this tank can take on all kinds of targets, from the lightest infantry to heavy assault vehicles.

This tank is very similar to the Prowler, save that there's one less gunner. A single gunner controls both of the Vanguard's main weapons systems, switching between them as desired.

The lone 150mm Cannon deals equivalent damage to the Prowler's two 100mm Cannons when both weapons systems are fired at a target over time. The Vanguard holds a slight edge in its ability to deal all its damage in single, concentrated shots.

The Prowler is a two-gunner tank, while the Vanguard has a single gunner. A Prowler with two gunners can fire both weapons systems simultaneously, while the Vanguard's lone gunner has to choose a system. It's a tradeoff between manpower and firepower; neither vehicle has the clear edge.

MAGRIDER (VS)

Top Speed: 60

Acceleration: 3

Maneuverability: 3

Total Armor: 2,500

Threshold: 10

Gunners: 1

Passengers: —

Weapons: Rail Beam, Pulse Accelerator

Weapon Type: Rail Beam

Damage Type: Direct

Vs. Infantry: 75

Vs. Vehicles: 200

Vs. Aircraft: 200

Weapon Type: Pulse Accelerator

Damage Type: Direct

Vs. Infantry: 20

Vs. Vehicles: 20

Vs. Aircraft: 40

The MagRider is a heavy hover-tank. It carries a heavy Rail Beam for anti-vehicle tasks and a fast-firing Pulse Accelerator for anti-infantry attacks. It's not as heavy and durable as other heavy tanks, but it can strafe thanks to its hover capabilities. This makes it extra-mobile and difficult to hit.

The MagRider can cross water for a limited time. Be sure not to be over water when the air jets run dry, or you'll sink.

The MagRider is slightly less powerful than the other two heavy tanks; its primary weapon deals damage similar to one of the Prowler's 100mm Cannons, but the dual 100mm Cannons fire somewhat faster than the MagRider's lone Rail Beam. As a result, the MagRider inflicts less damage over time.

The bottom line is that you must use the MagRider's unique ability to strafe and move laterally to dodge a few shots and make up for its slight lack of weapon power.

LAND TRANSPORTS

Transports aren't the flashiest of vehicles, but they serve a valuable purpose. They move players that would otherwise have a hard time traveling long distances and keep them together in the meantime. Their built-in weapons allow a squad to fend off attackers that might otherwise distract and divide the unit.

DELIVERER

Top Speed: 75

Acceleration: 3

Maneuverability: 3

Total Armor: 2,000

Threshold: 7

Gunners: 2

Passengers: 2

Weapons: 2 20mm Chainguns

Weapon Type: 20mm Chaingun

Damage Type: Direct

Vs. Infantry: 20

Vs. Vehicles: 20

Vs. Aircraft: 40

The Deliverer seats five, including a driver, two gunners that each man a 20mm Chaingun on a turret, and two passengers. Its armor and weaponry are not awe-inspiring, but it's effective at repelling infantry and light vehicle attacks. It's also pretty fast for a transport.

The Deliverer is amphibious. It moves very slowly in water, but it *can* cross; this opens up lots of possibilities on maps with water.

A squad can effectively move across the map with a single Deliverer, an AMS, and a couple of tanks.

SUNDERER

Top Speed: 70
Acceleration: 1
Maneuverability: 2
Total Armor: 3,500
Threshold: 10
Gunners: 2
Passengers: 6 (2 of them are MAX slots)

Weapons: 2 75mm Cannons
Weapon Type: 75mm Cannon
Damage Type: Explosive
Vs. Infantry: 40
Vs. Vehicles: 75
Vs. Aircraft: 75

The Sunderer is a massive ground transport, capable of carrying a driver, two MAXes, six regular passengers, and two gunners (11 people total). Each gunner mans a 75mm Cannon on a turret, which is good against vehicles and reasonably good against infantry, too. The vehicle isn't particularly fast, but it's very well armored and has more total armor than even the heaviest tanks.

The Sunderer is the ultimate land-based people transporter. Its ability to move more than an entire squad, extreme durability, and good weapons make it an excellent land-based alternative to the Galaxy.

NOTE

A Galaxy is usually faster and more efficient at people-moving than a Sunderer, especially on rough maps. However, consider that the Galaxy is only available at DropShip Centers and your Sanctuary, while a Sunderer can be purchased from any base if you control a Tech Plant on the continent.

AIR UNITS

There are only three air vehicles in *PlanetSide*, and all three perform distinct roles. Here's a look at them.

MOSQUITO

Top Speed: 120

Acceleration: 4

Maneuverability: 5

Total Armor: 500

Threshold: 0

Gunners: —

Passengers: —

Weapons: 12mm Chaingun

Weapon Type: 12mm Chaingun

Damage Type: Direct

Vs. Infantry: 25

Vs. Vehicles: 10

Vs. Aircraft: 25

The Mosquito is perhaps the ultimate scout and rapid transport vehicle. It allows a player to travel very quickly (faster than any other vehicle) and get a top-down view of the area. Also, it has a built-in ability to detect enemy units below and place them on the Proximity View map of you and your teammates. Enemy detection ability is based on the Mosquito's speed (50% or slower). The slower the Mosquito is moving, the more effective it is at detecting enemy soldiers and vehicles.

The Mosquito is also a stealthy vehicle. Like the Wraith and AMS, it very seldom shows up on enemy Proximity View—even when it's in range of an enemy Interlink Facility. As a result of its stealth, it never has to worry about taking fire from unmanned Wall Turrets.

While the Mosquito has a 12mm Chaingun (rotary), it's not great versus ground targets. It is an excellent dogfighter, though, and can usually outmaneuver and destroy Reavers. You can also use it to harass infantry, though you need to avoid heavy anti-vehicle weapons.

Again, it must be stressed that this is the fastest vehicle in existence. Its raw speed combined with its ability to fly over obstacles makes it a great choice for impatient players, who like to get places *fast*.

NOTE

Most players choose Reavers over Mosquitoes, due to the Reaver's heavier armor and weapons—but did we mention that Mosquitoes can usually take down Reavers in a dogfight?

REAVER

Top Speed: 105

Acceleration: 3

Maneuverability: 3

Total Armor: 900

Threshold: 5

Gunners: —

Passengers: —

Weapons: 2 Rocket Pods, 2 20mm Chainguns

Weapon Type: Rocket Pod

Damage Type: Explosive

Vs. Infantry: 35

Vs. Vehicles: 75

Vs. Aircraft: 75

Weapon Type: 20mm Chaingun

Damage Type: Direct

Vs. Infantry: 20

Vs. Vehicles: 20

Vs. Aircraft: 25

The Reaver is a powerful air-to-ground attack gunship. It's capable of harassing and destroying both infantry and vehicles, and its speedy flight characteristics allow it to get quickly from one place to another.

The Reaver has twin 20mm Chainguns and twin Rocket Pods. The rockets are best for anti-vehicle tasks, while the chaingun is ideal for dealing with infantry.

NOTE

The Reaver has an afterburner that can be engaged for short speed bursts. Don't forget this, as it's useful for combat, quick escapes, and even speeding up transit from one place to another.

The Reaver has a decent Threshold value, which makes it hard to destroy with infantry bullet weapons. However, it is very vulnerable to vehicles' bullet weapons, and Mosquitoes often have the upper hand in an aerial dogfight.

GALAXY

Top Speed: 80

Acceleration: 1

Maneuverability: 1

Total Armor: 5,000

Threshold: 7

Gunners: 3

Passengers: 8 (6 standard, 2 MAXes)

Weapons: 3 20mm Chainguns

Weapon Type: 20mm Chaingun

Damage Type: Direct

Vs. Infantry: 20

Vs. Vehicles: 20

Vs. Aircraft: 40

The Galaxy is *PlanetSide*'s ultimate people-mover. If you're planning a massive attack and want to ensure that everyone gets there quickly (and at the same time), your best policy is often to gather them at a DropShip Center and herd them into a Galaxy.

You can drive a small vehicle and its passengers into the Galaxy's cargo hold. Permitted vehicles include the Basilisk, Wraith, Harasser, Lightning, ANT, and all three Empire-specific assault buggies. The most common techniques are to pack an assault buggy for extra firepower when you land or an ANT so you can easily recharge captured facilities.

NOTE

If you pack a three-person assault buggy into a Galaxy, you can actually fit 15 people onboard—the pilot, three gunners, eight passengers, and the three buggy passengers.

The Galaxy has three 20mm Chainguns, each mounted on a turret in a different part of the vehicle. The Galaxy is also heavily armored—in fact, it's the most heavily armored thing on the planet. Though sluggish for an air vehicle, it's still faster than most land vehicles. Also, it doesn't need to worry about difficult terrain features.

The Galaxy has a few downsides. One is that it's only available at DropShip Centers and Sanctuaries. Another is that it's a big target that draws lots of attention. It's durable enough to withstand one heck of a beating, but if you get enough anti-aircraft weapons firing at it simultaneously, it will eventually go up in flames.

In the end, however, you can't go wrong with the Galaxy. It's the best option for moving lots of people safely and quickly.

CHAPTER 5: HOW THINGS WORK— TERMINALS, GADGETS, AND EMPLACED DEVICES

This chapter is devoted to explaining gadgets and devices, such as Equipment Terminals, Nano Dispensers, Spitfire Turrets, Command Consoles, and other such gear. In addition to physical gear, we'll discuss behind-the-scenes game mechanics that affect your character. For example: How close must you be to a facility to receive messages about its status (e.g., whether it's been hacked, or whether the Generator is under attack). From what distance can a Motion Detector detect you? What devices can you hack, and how long will it take?

Understanding this stuff is important; you won't become an effective player until you're familiar with the nuances of how the game world works. By the time you're done with this chapter you'll have a much better idea.

BASE OBJECTS

Facilities (a.k.a. bases) are not just inanimate buildings. They contain a wide array of devices that provide useful services.

TERMINALS

Terminals provide items or services. Approach them and activate them with the Action key (default G).

Terminals may be hacked. See the "Hacking" section at the end of this chapter for more information on what can be hacked, how long it takes, and what the effects are.

Terminals may also be destroyed. Usually, you only want to destroy terminals if you can't achieve your objectives some other way—say, by destroying a Generator or capturing an opponent's base outright. The latter methods are quicker and more efficient, and you don't have to individually repair a lot of terminals when you finally take over the base.

EQUIPMENT TERMINAL

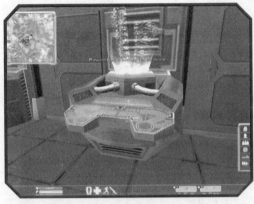

The Equipment Terminal is where you get your gear. Double-click on various items to add them to your inventory—or drag them, if you want to decide exactly where to place them.

Equipment Terminals appear in every base type, every tower, and in various structures in each Empire's Sanctuary. Also, an Equipment Terminal appears on the back of a deployed AMS.

Several people can use the same Equipment Terminal at once; it doesn't matter if someone else is standing there. Just get close to it, press your Action key (default [G]), and you can use it.

Equipment Terminals are crucial. Lockers allow you to store and retrieve items and weapons, but not armor—only Equipment Terminals dispense armor. Since newly respawned players start out in a Standard Exosuit (which provides a limited inventory and almost zero protection), it's crucial to have a friendly base or AMS conveniently at hand.

Despite their value, destroying Equipment Terminals is uncommon. Usually, the most effective way to disable enemy Equipment Terminals is to destroy the Generator of their facility, or destroy the AMS they're attached to.

It's much more common to hack Equipment Terminals than destroy them. Hacked Equipment Terminals can be a great asset during a base raid. If your whole squad knows about the hack, everyone can gather equipment—even inside an enemy-controlled base! Just realize that you may need to re-hack a terminal after the base status changes (for example, when the base goes from enemy-controlled to neutral during a base hack).

NOTE

Interestingly, a hacked enemy Equipment Terminal provides *your* Empire's gear when you access it. In other words, a Terran Republic player accessing a hacked Equipment Terminal will get access to Terran Republic guns (Cycler, Mini-Chaingun, etc.), regardless of the Empire controlling the facility.

You can create lists of your favorite weapon and armor packages and then select those favorites from any Equipment Terminal with a single click. Take some time to do this before you dive into the action; it's the only efficient way to equip yourself in battle.

VEHICLE TERMINAL

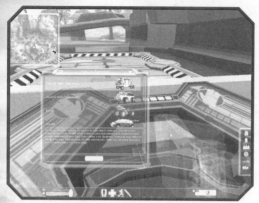

Vehicle Terminals are, as you might imagine, where you purchase *PlanetSide*'s various land and air vehicles.

Many facilities (Amp Stations, Bio Labs, Interlink Facilities) have a single, outdoor Vehicle Terminal somewhere in their courtyard. These facilities' Vehicle Terminals can only produce light vehicles, unless you own a Tech Plant on the same continent. If a Tech Plant is owned on the same continent, these facilities can produce all vehicles except the Galaxy transport.

NOTE

Time limits prevent you from buying a vehicle if you just purchased one in the last few minutes. The actual time restriction varies from vehicle to vehicle. If this restriction didn't exist, there would be less reason to, say, shoot down a Reaver—because you know its pilot could be up and flying again in a new Reaver, in just a few short moments.

DropShip Centers' Vehicle Terminals behave just like those of other facilities, except that you can always get a Galaxy in addition to the other available vehicles.

Tech Plants feature separate Vehicle Terminals for land and air vehicles. The land terminal is indoors, in the Tech Plant's subbasement. The air terminal is on the roof. Between these two Vehicle Terminals, Tech Plants can always produce *all* vehicles except for the Galaxy.

Sanctuaries have specialized land and air Vehicle Terminals, just like Tech Plants.

Vehicle Terminals can be hacked or destroyed. Hacking a Vehicle Terminal can be very powerful in a stealth-based attack; imagine dropping in near an unguarded enemy facility, hacking its Vehicle Terminal, buying an AMS, and deploying it right in the courtyard for an instant advantage.

Destroying Vehicle Terminals is a good policy in an all-out attack. Easy access to vehicles is one of the defenders' main assets, and taking that asset away can be a key to overrunning the base.

CERTIFICATION TERMINAL

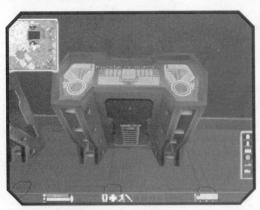

Certification Terminals are found in each Sanctuary's HART Shuttle Buildings and in Bio Labs. Certification Terminals are where you learn new Certifications for your character and unlearn old ones that you don't want anymore.

NOTE

Remember, if you unlearn more than one Certification, you must wait 24 hours before reclaiming Certification Points from the additional Certifications!

There's not a lot of complexity associated with these terminals. You'll typically only use them at the beginning or end of a play session, as that's when you're most likely to implement major character changes.

While these terminals may be hacked or even destroyed, there's usually not much incentive to do either. Instant access to Certifications is not your first priority in the middle of a base raid; similarly, preventing the enemy from getting convenient Certifications is not a particularly devastating strategy!

MEDICAL TERMINALS

Medical Terminals repair health and armor.

Medical Terminals are handy for players defending a base and for players stopping by the base to re-equip before going outside again. In the field, Medical Terminals won't be handy—so look into carrying Medkits, learning a Medical Certification, or getting an Implant that helps restore health.

A typical base has a Medical Terminal somewhere on the ground floor and one near the Lockers and Respawn Tubes.

IMPLANT TERMINAL

Implant Terminals are found in Sanctuaries and Bio Labs. Step up and activate them to add or remove Implants from your character. Unlike Certifications, Implants can be freely added and removed (with no wait or penalty if you change your mind).

As with other terminals, Implant Terminals can be hacked or destroyed—but these aren't particularly useful moves. Managing your Implants is usually something reserved for the beginning or end of a play session.

NOTE

There are occasionally times when you might use a hacked Implant Terminal to good effect. For example, after hacking an enemy Bio Lab (or any base), be alert for stealthy hackers targeting the Command Console. If you decide that your team isn't properly equipped to see them, you could hack an Implant Terminal and swap out your current Implant for Darklight Vision.

OTHER FACILITY DEVICES

There are more devices in a typical facility than terminals. Here's a look at the remaining gear.

MATRIX PANEL

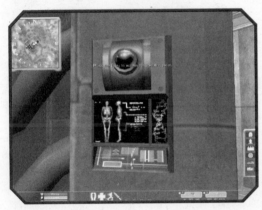

Matrix Panels are where you manually bind your character. They're found in facilities, towers, and on deployed AMSes.

When you're gunned down, you always have a selection of places to respawn. Your selection is improved if you've manually bound to Matrix Panels.

If you never bind to Matrix Panels, your selection is limited to the nearest deployed AMS, the nearest uncontested tower or facility, and your Empire's Sanctuary. If you're bound to Matrix Panels, however, you may add one additional AMS and one additional tower or facility to that list.

You can only bind to one particular AMS and to your choice of one tower or facility at one time. For example, if you bind to one AMS and then bind to a second AMS, you lose the first binding. Or, if you bind to a certain tower and then bind at a friendly facility, you lose the tower binding.

Also, realize that manual binding *doesn't* increase your options if you're gunned down right next to the vehicle or facility you're manually bound to. For example, let's say you bind to an AMS and then get sniped while you're standing right next to it. You're now allowed to respawn at the nearest friendly AMS or to the AMS you've bound to (in addition to the nearest facility and the facility you're bound to). However, since the AMS you bound to *is* the nearest AMS, that's the only AMS choice you're given.

So, the most useful binding points are close to the area where you plan to fight but not actually at that site. Binding at spots that fit that description lets you take advantage of any nearby respawn spots, while maintaining a backup plan.

COMMAND CONSOLE

The Command Console (sometimes called the control terminal) is the nerve center of a facility. To capture the facility, the Command Console must be hacked.

After the Command Console is hacked, there's a 15-minute transition period in which the base turns neutral and no equipment or terminals associated with the base may be used by anyone (unless they're individually hacked as well).

A small crossed flags icon appears under the facility name on the Tactical Map during the hacking period. The color of the crossed flags indicates which Empire hacked the base.

If the Empire that originally owned the base manages to re-hack the Command Console during the 15-minute transition period, the base *instantly* reverts to that Empire's control. If the 15 minutes passes uneventfully, however, the hacking Empire assumes control.

The Command Console is (naturally) a defensive focal point. When a base comes under attack, it's common to pack multiple defenders near the Console in an effort to repel the invasion with sheer numbers.

GENERATOR

Every base or facility has a Generator. Towers and Sanctuaries, however, do not. Generators power all the electronic gear (terminals, Matrix Panels, etc.) associated with their base. If the Generator is destroyed, all that gear loses power until it's repaired.

A message is broadcast throughout the facility's SOI when someone attacks a Generator. When a base loses power, a lightning bolt icon appears beneath it in Tactical View.

If resistance is light or nonexistent, it's usually better to take over a base without destroying the Generator; that way you don't need to repair it later. However, if resistance is heavy, destroying the Generator is often a great way of turning the odds in your favor. Without the ability to respawn or collect new equipment, the defenders will lose much of their edge.

NOTE

Taking down a Generator has no effect on the Command Console or on any hacks taking place at that Console. Command Consoles are independently powered.

RESPAWN TUBES

Respawn Tubes are located in all Sanctuaries, all facilities, and all towers. They also appear on deployed AMSes. Respawn Tubes are the devices that respawned players pop out of. Without them, no respawning can take place at that location.

Respawn Tubes can be destroyed, though it's more common to destroy a facility's Generator instead, thus killing power not only to the Respawn Tubes but also to all other base equipment. However, if the defenders are particularly good at protecting their Generator, or if you have an easy shot at the Respawn Tubes, attack the tubes instead.

One benefit of attacking the tubes instead of the Generator: While power outages are immediately apparent, the enemy is much less likely to notice when you destroy Respawn Tubes. This allows you to disable key facilities without alerting the defense that something is going wrong.

NOTE

Sometimes players camp near enemy Respawn Tubes, gunning down anyone who pops out. While this is an effective way of dealing with respawning enemies, you won't get many BEPs (Battlefield Experience Points) for these kills. Newly respawned players are nearly helpless, and the game takes that into account.

LOCKERS

Lockers, despite the mundane name, are high-tech devices. When you pack gear into a Locker, you can later open any Locker, *anywhere*, and grab that gear from it.

Lockers should be stocked as a contingency plan for times when Equipment Terminals are destroyed or unpowered. They can't store armor, so they're no substitute for Equipment Terminals, but it's nice having them stocked for the few occasions when you really need some gear.

NOTE

If you have the Engineering skill, always stock your locker with a Nano Dispenser. Without this precaution, it's difficult to repair a base with a destroyed Generator (because the Equipment Terminals aren't working, so you can't just buy a Nano Dispenser).

PHALANX TURRETS (A.K.A. WALL TURRETS)

Wall Turrets dot the walls of every facility. They also appear atop Air Towers and Gun Towers.

Wall Turrets automatically fire at most enemy vehicles if you possess an Interlink Facility on the continent. (When cloaked, they never fire at a deployed AMS, a Wraith, or a Mosquito.)

Players in Standard or Agile Exosuits can climb into Wall Turrets and fire them manually. When manned by a skilled player, these turrets are lethal against both vehicles and infantry. They have a high rate of fire and deal excellent damage.

Damage to a Wall Turret does not pass through to a player manning it, though the player is killed if the turret gets destroyed.

Wall Turrets have self-regenerating shields if you control an Amp Station somewhere on the continent. These shields make the turrets much harder to destroy.

When approaching an enemy base in a vehicle, watch out for Wall Turrets. If they're manned, or if they're controlled by an Interlink Facility, hang back and take down some of the turrets before venturing in with your vehicle.

NTU SILO

Every base has a silo where its NTUs are stored. An indicator on the front of the silo tells you how full it is. To stock up a base with NTUs, drive an ANT up to the silo and deploy it. (Be sure the ANT has been charged up first!)

HANDHELD DEVICES

The following handheld devices may be purchased at an Equipment Terminal.

REMOTE ELECTRONICS KIT (REK)

The REK is necessary for all types of hacking. Since everyone can hack a door or Command Console, this pistol-sized device should be taken by most characters. Only players in MAX armor (who can't equip it) have no use for it.

Hacking is accomplished by pointing the REK at the object to be hacked and pressing the Fire button. A beam shoots from the REK and a status bar shows the progress of the hack. You can let go of the button when the bar appears; your character automatically keeps hacking.

TIP

We recommend switching to third-person perspective while hacking. This gives you a bit of warning if an enemy sneaks up behind you; if that happens, break off the hack by pressing the Fire button again, and try to fight or escape.

Refer to the "Hacking" section at the end of this chapter for more information on what you can hack and how long it takes.

MEDKIT

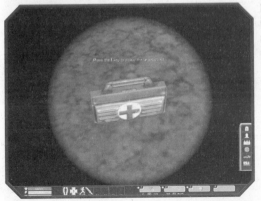

Medkits may be used by any character; they instantly heal 25 points of health. There's a several-second waiting period after each use, so you can't quickly tap a key and use multiple Medkits in an instant.

MEDICAL APPLICATOR

The pistol-sized Medical Applicator restores a player's health. In its primary fire mode, it heals a target at close range; in secondary fire mode, it heals the user. Healing takes place gradually.

Medical Applicators are powered by Health Canisters. When you run out of Health Canisters, the applicator cannot be used.

Medical Applicators may only be used by players with the Medical Certification. Players with the Advanced Medical Certification can use the Medical Applicator on recently killed allies to bring them back to life.

NOTE

Newly revived players have full health but reduced stamina and armor, so reviving them in the middle of a firefight is usually a pointless endeavor; they're likely to get mowed down again by a stray bullet. Revive teammates after you've won a skirmish, or whenever there's a lull in the action.

BODY ARMOR NANO KIT (BANK)

The pistol-sized Body Armor Nano Kit (BANK) repairs armor. In its primary fire mode it repairs the armor of the target it's pointed at; in its secondary mode it repairs the user's armor.

BANKs are powered by Armor Canisters. When the Armor Canisters run dry, the BANK can no longer be used.

BANKs may only be used by players with the Engineering Certification.

NANO DISPENSER

The Nano Dispenser is a rifle-sized device that can repair vehicles or objects (such as Respawn Tubes, Generators, and various terminals). Just point it at a nearby target and fire.

The Nano Dispenser is powered by Armor Canisters, just like the BANK. When the Armor Canisters run out, you can no longer use the Nano Dispenser.

COMMAND UPLINK DEVICE

The pistol-sized Command Uplink Device may only be selected and carried by characters who have achieved Command Rank 2 or higher.

The exact functions of the Command Uplink Device are based on the user's Command Rank. Refer to chapter 7 for detailed information on this device.

ENGINEER DEVICES

These objects are created when a character with the Combat Engineering Certification uses an Adaptive Construction Engine (ACE) device. The ACE is used up in the creation of the object.

While none of these devices can defend a base on their own, they're great for supplementing human defenses.

MOTION SENSORS

Motion Sensors detect enemy vehicles and soldiers within 50 meters, if they are moving faster than 3.5 meters per second. Detected enemies appear on the Proximity View maps of all friendly units in the area.

Motion Sensors may be deployed anywhere but inside the SOI (Sphere of Influence) of enemy facilities. An Engineer can place 20 Motion Sensors in a friendly Sphere of Influence. They can be stuck to angled surfaces, so you have lots of choices when placing them. Try to conceal them as much as possible, so the enemy doesn't see them and destroy them. It's also common practice to place them near Spitfire Turrets; enemies tend to go after the turrets first, which buys a few more seconds of detection time for the Motion Sensor.

Motion Sensors, like all deployable devices, have a lockout radius. You can't place other Motion Sensors inside that radius; this prevents you from placing ridiculous numbers of them in one particular spot.

NOTE

If you place more than 20 Motion Sensors in a particular Sphere of Influence, the first one you placed is automatically removed as you place the 21st. You can keep deploying them, but old ones are constantly removed, so you've never got more than 20 in that SOI. The same thing happens when you exceed the limit on other deployable items.

NOTE

The limit of 20 Motion Sensors per Sphere of Influence is for each Engineer; it's not an absolute for the entire SOI. So, one Engineer could place 20 Motion Sensors in an SOI, and his friend could place another 20—*if* they could find spots to put them all.

NOTE

Frequently checking Proximity View is always a good idea, since it allows you to see where nearby friendly units are. The addition of enemy units, thanks to Motion Sensors, provides another excellent reason to make constant use of Proximity View.

All armor types move at 3.5 meters per second, or faster, when running. All armor types move slower than 3.5 meters per second when walking or crouch-walking. Therefore, to avoid a Motion Sensor, walk or crouch-walk.

If you encounter Motion Sensors in a situation where you aren't concerned about being seen, either run right past them or, better yet, destroy them. Blasting a few shots of armor-piercing ammunition at close range usually does the trick.

SPITFIRE TURRETS

Spitfire Turret

Spitfire Turrets are small, automated turrets that fire at running enemies detected within 50 meters. If you fire at them, they'll return fire (with surprisingly good accuracy) at any distance.

Just like Motion Sensors, Spitfire Turrets detect (and fire at) all enemies moving faster than 3.5 meters per second. So you can avoid their attention by walking or crouch-walking.

If you shoot a Spitfire Turret, it briefly returns fire, even if you are not running. This is its automated defense system in action.

Spitfire Turrets, like Motion Sensors, may be deployed anywhere but in an enemy facility's SOI. Each Engineer can pack 10 of them into a friendly SOI; deploying an eleventh Spitfire in an SOI causes the first one to be removed. They must be deployed on a flat surface, and they can't be placed inside the lockout radius of another Spitfire.

The two main ways of destroying a Spitfire Turret are to take it out from a distance, using cover, or to get up very close. When taking it out from a distance, use anti-vehicle weapons or fire bursts of armor-piercing ammo. Then briefly duck behind cover while the turret returns fire. Repeat until the turret is gone.

CAUTION

Spitfire Turrets can fire accurately at ranges *much* greater than 50 meters; that's only the radius in which they'll open fire on their own. Just because you're out of the turret's normal firing range, don't assume that there won't be any return fire.

To take out a Spitfire Turret from close range, walk or crouch-walk right up to it. Get behind it, crouch for accuracy, and blast it with a nonstop stream of armor-piercing bullets. You'll probably take a small amount of damage, but you'll quickly annihilate the turret.

The very worst thing you can do when facing a Spitfire Turret is to open fire from medium range with no cover (or run past it at medium range with no cover). It's very accurate at this range, whereas you need to crouch and fire in short bursts to maintain your accuracy. You'll suffer serious damage if you take on a Spitfire Turret this way.

HE MINES

HE Mines become live once they are deployed. They automatically detonate whenever an enemy gets close to them (within a meter or so). The explosion is usually not enough to kill an armored player outright, though unarmored enemies (e.g., those in Infiltration Suits or Standard Exosuits) generally perish in the blast.

Mines laid by a member of your Empire will not detonate when you walk on them. These mines have a green ring around them—so you can easily determine whether a mine is a threat just by looking at it.

Each Engineer can lay up to 20 active mines in a given SOI. When they lay the 21st mine, the oldest mine they laid disappears.

HE Mines have a lockout radius. Other mines cannot be placed within this radius. This prevents players from building minefield deathtraps that are a huge pain to deal with.

HE Mines may be placed in an enemy SOI, but they may never be placed indoors (even in friendly territory).

Enemy mines can be harmlessly cleared by throwing a Jammer Grenade in their general vicinity. You can also shoot them, though this requires good aim or a weapon with a blast radius. They're harder to hit than they look!

Effective spots for mines include: right in front of doorways leading inside (remember, they can't be placed inside), near base entrances, at the foot of a stairwell, or at the top of a stairwell. Other, more random spots are less tactical but can score cheap kills, because players won't be looking for mines in unusual places.

If you're infiltrating a base, avoid mines (best if you're lightly armored and trying to sneak in), detonate them with Jammer Grenades or live fire, or simply bite the bullet and take your damage. The last option is useful when a mine is preventing a large attack force from entering a key area; in such cases, it can be better for one player to immediately charge in and take the damage, rather than hanging back and letting the enemy pick your group apart.

BOOMER HE

The Boomer HE is like an extra-powerful HE Mine, except that it doesn't detonate automatically. When you drop a Boomer it generates a detonator; equip the detonator and press the Fire button (default left-click) to explode the Boomer.

The chief advantage of the Boomer is that it can be placed just about anywhere, including indoors and inside an enemy SOI.

It's possible to deploy multiple Boomers and have multiple detonators, but it's tough keeping them straight and awkward switching the right one in and out of your hands. It's best to lay just one or two.

Boomers are good for defensive situations. They make good booby traps when you're guarding a Command Console, and they can also be useful at the back door or main gate of a facility. You need to watch them with the detonator in your hand for them to be useful, though, so it's tricky to use them hand-in-hand with guns.

Like mines, friendly Boomers have a green ring that lets you immediately tell if they're friend or foe. Unlike mines, Boomers are always controlled by players—so watch out for allies with overly twitchy trigger fingers.

If you see an enemy Boomer on the ground, stay away from it and immediately scour the area for hiding enemies. Turn on Darklight Vision if you've got it. There's a good chance you'll find a lurking enemy with a detonator in hand—and score an extremely easy and satisfying kill!

DISTANCE AND SOI (SPHERE OF INFLUENCE) MECHANICS

A number of important game mechanics are based on distance and proximity. While these mechanics are not technically gadgets or devices, understanding them is just as important as understanding how various devices work. That's why they're covered here.

PLAYER COMMUNICATION RANGE

Most chat modes (Squad, Outfit, Alliance) work regardless of distance. However, a couple of modes are distance-related.

Open chat (select "Open" from the list atop the chat window, or preface your typed statements with /open) shows your statements to everyone within 200 meters.

Broadcast chat (preface with /b) goes out to everyone in your Empire in the same facility SOI or Sanctuary. You can't use this mode in an enemy SOI.

These modes are useful for finding squads and clueing in nearby allies on important information (such as the arrival of an enemy Galaxy).

RANGE OF GAME-GENERATED MESSAGES

The capture of a facility or tower is broadcast across the entire continent; everyone on that continent gets the message. These are the *only* standard game-generated messages that are broadcast continent-wide.

Kill messages (i.e., messages telling you who killed whom) are broadcast over a short distance (about 200 meters) when you're away from a facility's SOI. When you're inside a SOI, you'll get all kill messages within the SOI. Watch these color-coded messages; over time you'll get a sense of who's winning most of the battles.

Facility-related messages (aside from control changes) are only broadcast to players within that facility's SOI. These include "hacked" (e.g., "The Vanu Sovereignty has hacked into Bio Lab X.") and "Generator attacked" (e.g., "Technology Center Y's Generator is under attack.") messages.

NOTE

Keep a close eye on the continent map and watch for the little crossed flags icon that represents a hack in progress. That's the only way you'll know if the enemy has hacked one of your distant facilities (unless someone tells you about it).

RECEIVING EXPERIENCE FROM SQUAD ACTIONS

The original design specification called for characters to only receive experience from squad members' actions if those squad members were within 200 meters. However, this was eventually changed, as it discouraged activities that took squad members away from the group (such as scouting or grabbing an ANT). Now you receive experience from capturing bases as long as you're on the same continent they're on.

DEPLOYING ITEMS

As previously noted, deployable items generate an interference field that prevents placement of identical items within a certain distance. Mines have a 10-meter interference field; Boomers have a much smaller field (only a few meters). Spitfire Turrets and Motion Sensors have a 20-meter interference field.

HACKING

Hacking is a big part of *PlanetSide*. Here are a few notes on what you can hack, how long it takes, and precisely what effect hacking has. Understanding how these things work is crucial, even if you don't plan to be a hacker.

EFFECTS OF HACKING

When you hack a base's Command Console, the base automatically becomes neutral for a 15-minute period, during which the base will *instantly* revert to its former Empire if a member of that Empire manages to re-hack the Console. If you can defend the hacked Console for that time period, the base transfers to your Empire's control.

Hacking vehicles makes you the new owner. Both you and all members of your Empire can now use these vehicles, just as if they were purchased at a Vehicle Terminal. You need Certifcation to drive them.

Hacking individual terminals (such as Medical Terminals and Equipment Terminals) removes the IFF (Identify Friend or Foe) protection. Once hacked, that terminal can be used by anyone from any Empire. The terminal simply loses its ability to tell who is accessing it.

WHAT YOU CAN HACK

In addition to Command Consoles, any player may hack a door lock.

Players with the Hacking skill may additionally hack any terminal or vehicle.

NOTE

Look up to hack an Implant Terminal. That's where all the electronics are.

HACK SPEED

Here's a list that ranks the hack speed for various objects and vehicles. The first objects on the list can be hacked very quickly; the last ones take a long time. The exact time it takes depends on your level of hacking skill (no Certifications, Hacking Certification, or Advanced Hacking Certification).

- Doors and Medical Terminals
- Lockers and all other terminals
- Most vehicles
- AMSes
- Command Consoles

Someone without any Hacking Certifications will spend 10 to 15 seconds opening a door lock, while someone with Advanced Hacking will burn through locks in two seconds flat. Similarly, while a non-hacker will take a couple minutes to hack a Command Console, an Advanced Hacker can get the job done in less than 30 seconds.

Here's a more detailed table that just covers vehicles. Again, it starts with the quickest hacks and moves on to the longest:

- Basilisk, Wraith
- Harasser
- Enforcer, Lightning, Marauder, Mosquito, Thresher
- Deliverer
- MagRider, Prowler, Reaver, Vanguard
- Sunderer
- Galaxy
- AMS

Just to give you a sense of scale, it takes someone with the standard Hacking Certification about 10 seconds to jack a Basilisk or Wraith; an AMS would take about 60 seconds. Someone with Advanced Hacking can grab a Basilisk or Wraith in about 3 seconds, and an AMS in about 20 seconds.

As you can see, hacking an AMS or any large vehicle takes time, but it's worthwhile if you can manage it.

CHAPTER 6: AURAXIS™

Here's an overview of Auraxis™, including detailed information on Sanctuaries, Battle Continents, and the vital facilities that you'll be attacking and defending. You'll also find tips on getting from one place to another, plus information on important, planet-wide game systems.

SERVERS

When you start the game, you may have a choice of servers on which to play. Each game server hosts its own copy of the planet Auraxis™; all characters you create are unique to that server (in other words, you can't create a character on one server, then log onto a different server and expect to find him or her there).

Because of this, you'll typically select a server the first time you play and stick with it indefinitely. The server you pick should be the one that consistently delivers the lowest ping.

NOTE

Ping is a number representing the time it takes for data to flow between your computer and the server. Low ping is good; high ping means there's a substantial delay between when events happen in the game world and when you see them. A ping under 250 is manageable; below 200 is better, but you'll still be at a slight disadvantage until you can get down near 150. You can usually achieve a ping around 150 if you have a high-speed data connection.

WORLD MAP AND OVERVIEW

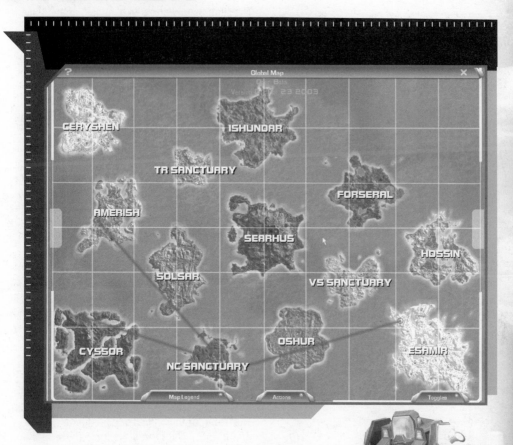

Auraxis™'s significant landmasses include three Sanctuaries and 10 Battle Continents. All of these are visible on your in-game map.

Access a view of the current continent or Sanctuary by pressing the Map key (M by default). Select the Global View option to get an overview of Auraxis™.

READING THE IN-GAME MAP (GLOBAL VIEW)

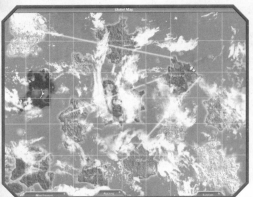

The Global View gives an overview of the game world and displays Warp Gate connections between continents; simply click on a continent to see all Warp Gate connections between it and the other continents.

Hot spots on the map show you the largest concentrations of conflict. These are places you might want to jump in and lend a hand—or avoid, if you want to play a sneakier game.

Storms are also quite evident from this view; they appear as large, partially shaded spheres. The size of the sphere is a rough approximation of the storm front's size, while the color is a general indicator of its severity (green is mild, red is harsh). The actual effects of the storm (rain, fog, snow) largely depend on the continent. Weather's effects in *PlanetSide* tend to be overlooked, though certain occurrences, like heavy rain and fog, can reduce the effectiveness of a sniper or airborne vehicle pilot, and improve the prospects of stealthy characters.

If you're in a squad, your squadmates' numbers appear on the Global View, indicating their current locations.

Most of the time, Global View functions as a selecting device. Double-click on any continent to zoom in on it; the zoomed-in mode is called the Tactical View, and that's where most of the real information is.

READING THE IN-GAME MAP (TACTICAL VIEW)

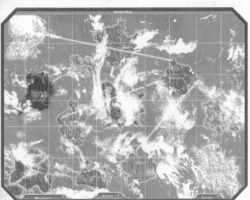

The Tactical View illustrates a single Battle Continent or Sanctuary. Multiple individual hot spots allow you to see where the heaviest fighting is taking place.

Weather patterns are visible on the Tactical View. Also, if you zoom in close enough, you can see individual deployed items (Spitfire Turrets, mines, etc.) in your current Sphere of Influence. They appear as small icons, roughly shaped like the deployable items themselves.

Squad members appear as numbers on the Tactical View—if, of course, you're looking at the right continent!

In addition to facilities, the Tactical Map displays the Continental Lattice. The Continental Lattice is a web of lines drawn between facilities; it shows you which enemy facilities you can currently hack.

Gold lines are your Empire's "attack lines"; they show you which facilities can be attacked. Gray lines show other Empires' attack options. Red, blue, and purple lines connect facilities owned by the same Empire; the color is determined by the Empire in charge (red for Terran Republic, blue for New Conglomerate, purple for Vanu Sovereignty).

The rule of thumb is: To attack a facility, you need to possess an adjacent facility. If you don't possess an adjacent facility, you need to capture one.

Facilities adjacent to one of your Empire's secure Warp Gates (i.e. Warp Gates connected directly to your Empire's Sanctuary) are always valid targets, even if you don't possess any facilities on that continent.

If a continent is locked, you need to pick a Warp Gate, locate the corresponding Warp Gate on a different continent, and capture facilities adjacent to that corresponding gate. When you've captured those facilities, a facility on the target continent (near the selected Warp Gate) will become valid.

You can toggle a great deal of information on or off; we recommend leaving most of it on, most of the time. Facility names, Spheres of Influence, and NTU levels are very important for getting a sense of how the battle is going. Also, watch for the little "crossed flags" icon that indicates a hacked facility and the "little lightning bolt" icon that represents a facility with a broken Generator. These icons let you know which of your facilities are in trouble and which of your opponents' facilities are under siege.

If you possess high enough Command Rank, you'll have access to information-gathering techniques that place even more information on this map. We'll explore this more in chapter 7, along with more information on Command Ranks and Battle Ranks.

THE PROXIMITY MAP

The Proximity Map (sometimes called radar) provides crucial information on your immediate surroundings. You can close it, but we strongly recommend leaving it open at all times and constantly referring to it. Failure to do so will put you at a great disadvantage by lowering your awareness of what's going on nearby.

WHAT THE PROXIMITY MAP SHOWS

The Proximity Map shows friendly soldiers and vehicles, enemy soldiers and vehicles, major terrain features, and even floor plans if you're inside a base.

Friendly soldiers appear as teal dots, while enemy soldiers are red. Squad members appear as numbers. MAXes show up as small bracket-shaped objects, while vehicles all have their own distinctive silhouettes. You'll come to recognize them all after playing for a few days.

Enemy vehicles and soldiers appear on the Proximity Map if you've got them in your view, if a nearby ally has them in view, or if they're detected by an Interlink Facility or Motion Detectors. Otherwise they don't show up at all—so don't interpret a Proximity Map with no red dots as an area free of enemies.

ZOOM LEVELS AND DETAILS

There are three zoom settings: 50, 100, and 200 meters. We recommend using the 50-meter setting indoors and the 200-meter setting most other times. (Occasionally you'll want to scale down to 100 meters to see more detail.)

The 50-meter setting is best indoors, because the floor plan of the facility is easy to read. Icons representing various important areas (Respawn Tubes, Equipment Terminals) also show up clearly at this setting.

Outside, you just want to see as much as possible. The 200-meter setting is great for, say, locating a friendly AMS or spotting enemies from a distance.

SANCTUARIES

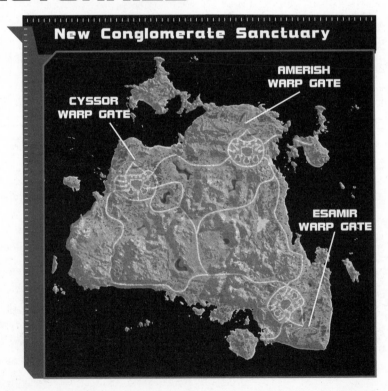

New Conglomerate Sanctuary

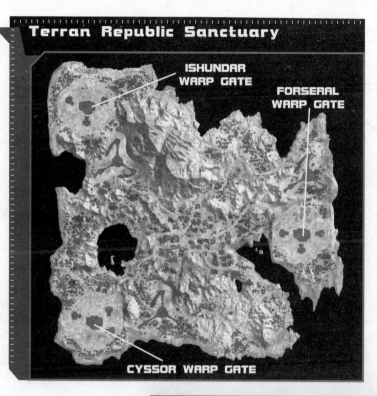

Terran Republic Sanctuary

ISHUNDAR
WARP GATE

FORSERAL
WARP GATE

CYSSOR WARP GATE

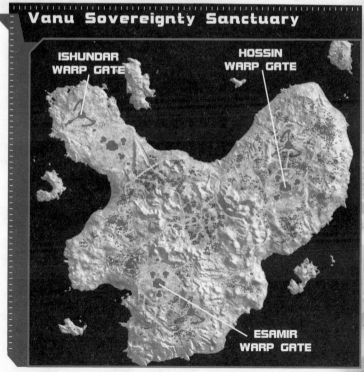

Vanu Sovereignty Sanctuary

ISHUNDAR
WARP GATE

HOSSIN
WARP GATE

ESAMIR
WARP GATE

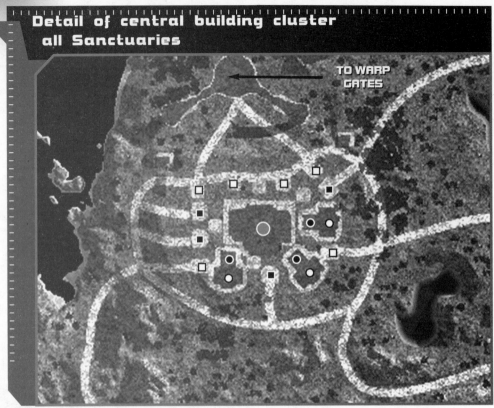

Detail of central building cluster all Sanctuaries

TO WARP GATES

- ○ RESPAWN CENTER
- ○ TRAINING CENTER
- ○ HART SHUTTLE BUILDING
- □ AIR VEHICLE TERMINAL
- ■ GROUND VEHICLE TERMINAL

The three Empires' Sanctuaries are virtually identical in form and function. The shape of each island is different, but each Sanctuary features a cluster of key structures next to each of its three Warp Gates. Small "teleportation pads" allow you to quickly move between the three building clusters. Refer to the Detail Map for an overview of one of these clusters.

NOTE

Check out the three Sanctuary maps, and then refer to the detail map for a closer look at the important buildings; remember, the detail map applies to all three Sanctuaries.

When you first play *PlanetSide*, resist the temptation to leap right into battle. Spend some time playing with the various facilities (especially the Virtual Training Center) at your Sanctuary.

Later, when you're more experienced, the Sanctuary is a useful place to meet people, assemble squads, modify and equip your character, and ship out to a combat site.

Here are a few notes on the various Sanctuary facilities.

RESPAWNING FACILITIES

You appear in the Respawning Facility's Respawn Tubes whenever you: first create a character; respawn to your Sanctuary (click on the Sanctuary respawn point in the bottom-right corner of the map screen, after dying); or select the Recall to Sanctuary option from the [esc] menu.

There are Equipment Terminals here, but no other facilities. To re-equip and get back into the action, use the Equipment Terminals and make a quick break for the door. To heal your character, add or remove Implants, or manage your Certifications, head straight for the HART Shuttle Buildings.

VIRTUAL TRAINING CENTER

The Virtual Training Center is attached to the respawning facilities and has two Zones: the Virtual Shooting Range and the Virtual Driving Zone.

You may initially find it silly that these facilities exist; after all, what's the point of playing a virtual reality game inside another game? However, the VR Zones allow you to test all weapons and all vehicles, regardless of what you're currently certified in. You won't get that opportunity elsewhere.

Weapons can be tested against various armor and vehicle types, giving you a pretty good sense of how they fare against different targets.

Virtual Reality Driving Zone

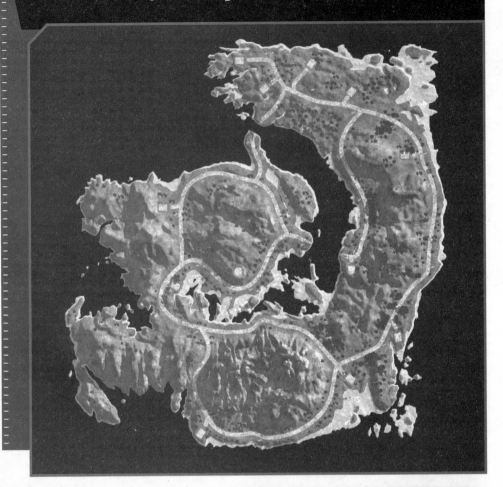

NOTE

If you want to test a vehicle with a gunner position, bring a friend to the Virtual Driving Zone.

We strongly recommend that you pay the VR Zones a short visit when you first create a character, just to acquaint yourself with the game's various weapons and vehicles. Later, when you have some Certification Points to spend, return and do some research on the weapons and vehicles you like best. Spending a few minutes here helps you avoid picking a Certification you don't want and enduring the day-long wait before you can reclaim the Certification Points.

HART SHUTTLE BUILDINGS

These buildings are where the HART Shuttles depart. Look for the doors with the timers up above; when the timers read zero, you can go inside and climb aboard a Shuttle. After a brief wait, you're sent up. Use the World Map to pick a destination, and you'll be dropped to the surface in a Drop Pod.

If the timer above the door shows anything but zero, you must wait for it to count down before entering. The Shuttle interval can (and probably will) be adjusted by the game designers, but it's long enough for Warp Gate travel.

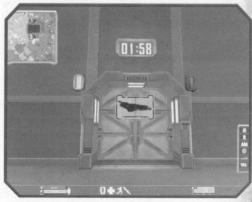

TIP

Though you may enter the Shuttle with other people, your process of selecting a drop location has no effect on anyone else. For example, two people can enter the Shuttle at the same time but drop on different continents. One of them might spend three minutes selecting a location, while the other almost instantaneously drops. Take as long as you want; nobody is affected if you spend a long time in orbit.

NOTE

Look for extra terminals upstairs.

The HART Shuttle Buildings also contain Equipment Terminals, Certification Terminals, Implant Terminals, Advanced Medical Terminals, and Lockers (they're tucked away; you have to look for them). This makes them one-stop destinations for everything you might need between missions.

LAND VEHICLE TERMINALS

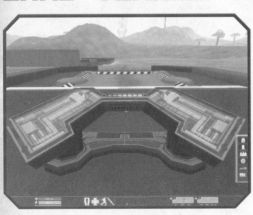

You can purchase any land vehicle at these outdoor Vehicle Terminals. Collect your vehicle, then head for the Warp Gates.

AIR VEHICLE TERMINALS

Only the Mosquito, the Reaver, and the massive Galaxy transport may be collected at these terminals. Buy a vehicle, grab some friends, and make for the Warp Gates!

WARP GATES

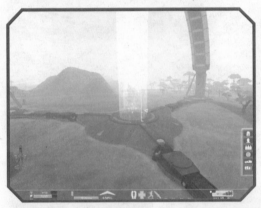

Sanctuary Warp Gates are the preferred method of getting to nearby Battle Continents. Getting to continents that aren't connected to your Sanctuary is more work; you'll need to refer to the Global View and plot a route that takes you through multiple Warp Gates. (Or, just use the HART Shuttle.)

Warp Gates are typically used to travel *away* from the Sanctuary, but seldom *to* it, as you can always just press esc and select Recall to Sanctuary for a quick ticket home.

BATTLE CONTINENTS

Auraxis™ features 10 Battle Continents. As the name suggests, these continents are the setting for all of PlanetSide's battles. Every continent contains a number of facilities and a handful of Warp Gates, but beyond that they're all quite different. The next few sections note the major differences between continents.

NOTE

The continent you're fighting on won't have much effect on individual battles, especially at close range or indoors. It will affect large-scale factors like the defensibility of a particular base, the feasibility of driving land vehicles across the map, or the relative ease or difficulty of hiding a large force.

AMERISH

Amerish is a temperate continent. The landmass is mostly contiguous, though a few islands connected by bridges provide alternate routes to key locations. One facility is even located on an island. This isn't particularly harsh terrain, so land vehicles are easy to use.

The facilities here are loosely grouped into a northern cluster and a southern cluster, with a large, empty (save for two Warp Gates) middle ground separating them. It's easiest to launch an attack if you already control a facility in the target's cluster (northern or southern). Without that kind of toehold, you're in for a tough fight.

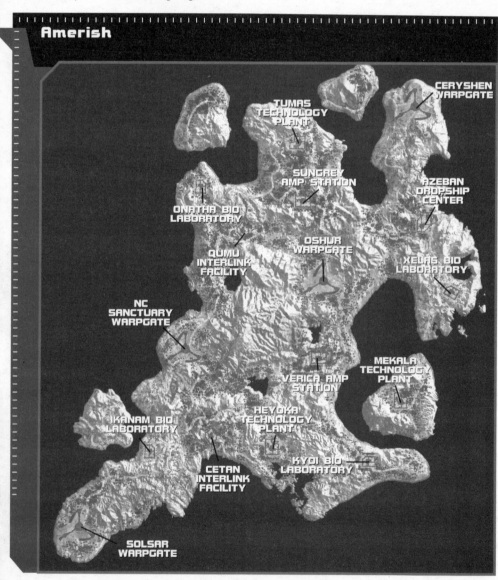

Amerish

CERYSHEN WARPGATE

TUMAS TECHNOLOGY PLANT

SUNGREY AMP STATION

AZEBAN DROPSHIP CENTER

ONATHA BIO LABORATORY

OSHUR WARPGATE

QUMU INTERLINK FACILITY

XELAS BIO LABORATORY

NC SANCTUARY WARPGATE

MEKALA TECHNOLOGY PLANT

VERICA AMP STATION

IKANAM BIO LABORATORY

HEYOKA TECHNOLOGY PLANT

KYOI BIO LABORATORY

CETAN INTERLINK FACILITY

SOLSAR WARPGATE

CERYSHEN

Ceryshen is a deceptive arctic continent. The big landmass and lack of bridges or islands may suggest an easy trek, but tall, impassable mountains dominate several parts of it. You can't just plunk a waypoint on the map and expect to take a straight path from one location to another; rather, you need to study the map and see what it allows. Often you'll need to take a convoluted route.

The difficult terrain of Ceryshen emphasizes the value of air vehicles. It also makes getting places on foot (or in slow vehicles) a tricky and time-consuming proposition. Getting killed without an AMS nearby can be heartbreaking, because you'll probably have to trek a long way just to return to the battlefield.

The terrain definitely favors defenders. Aside from the bright white snow, which offers little cover for attackers, the landscape barriers often force attackers into narrow, easy-to-observe routes.

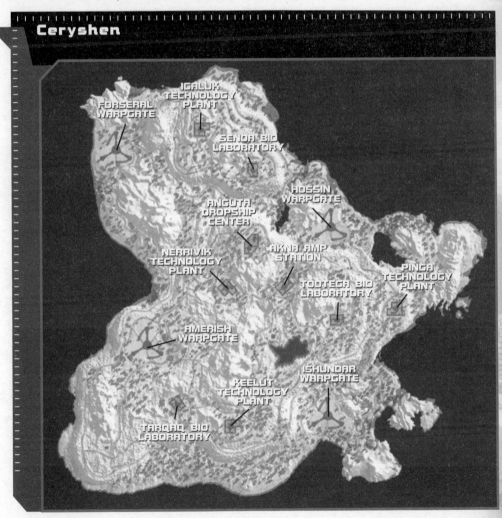

Ceryshen

FORSERAL WARPGATE

IGALUK TECHNOLOGY PLANT

SENDA BIO LABORATORY

HOSSIN WARPGATE

ANGUTA DROPSHIP CENTER

NERRIVIK TECHNOLOGY PLANT

AKNA AMP STATION

PINGA TECHNOLOGY PLANT

TOOTEGA BIO LABORATORY

AMERISH WARPGATE

ISHUNDAR WARPGATE

KEELUT TECHNOLOGY PLANT

TARQAQ BIO LABORATORY

PRIMA'S OFFICIAL STRATEGY GUIDE

CYSSOR

Cyssor is a broken continent, formed of many large pieces (and a few smaller ones). Bridges connect the land in various key spots.

The facilities on Cyssor are grouped into small clusters. The central cluster, which includes the Gunuku DropShip Center, is the most strategically valuable. Gunuku itself is very easy to defend, thanks to the deep water that surrounds it—but as the lone DropShip Center on the map, it's often contested.

Bridges are useful, but they can be deadly choke points. If the going gets rough, and the defenders load up their defenses at a particular bridge, look for a longer way around—even if it's time-consuming and inconvenient. Or, look to the Warp Gates or HART Shuttle as different points of entry to this fragmented continent.

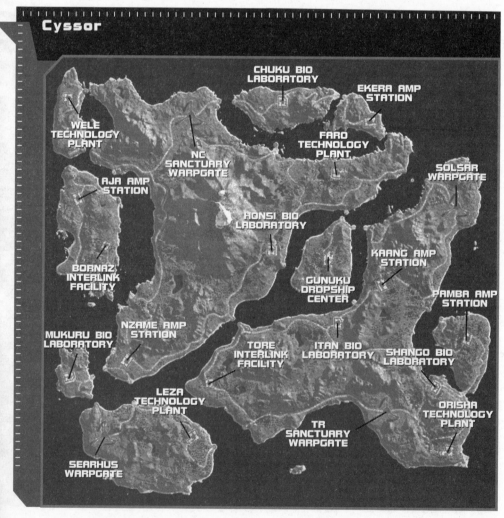

Cyssor

ESAMIR

Like Ceryshen, Esamir is an arctic continent. Unlike Ceryshen, Esamir features some water and bridges—chiefly in the north and in the map's center, where water rings a pair of key facilities.

While Esamir's terrain is not as mountainous as that of Ceryshen, it's still quite hilly and deceptive, and visibility is limited. Land vehicles are difficult to use here; air vehicles and infantry tend to do better. Plan your assaults well, and bring an extra AMS; you really don't want to cross this continent on foot!

The water on Esamir can be crossed, if you ford at the right spots. This is important for avoiding the often-guarded bridges.

Esamir

- NC SANCTUARY WARPGATE
- ANDUVARI DROPSHIP CENTER
- DAGUR TECHNOLOGY PLANT
- JARI INTERLINK FACILITY
- EISA TECHNOLOGY PLANT
- MANI BIO LABORATORY
- NOTT AMP STATION
- YMIR BIO LABORATORY
- FREYR AMP STATION
- OSHUR WARPGATE
- GUALLAR TECHNOLOGY PLANT
- HELHEIM TECHNOLOGY PLANT
- SEARHUS WARPGATE
- VIDAR INTERLINK FACILITY
- RAN BIO LABORATORY
- KVASIR AMP STATION
- VS SANCTUARY WARPGATE

PRIMA'S OFFICIAL STRATEGY GUIDE

FORSERAL

This temperate continent features Warp Gates at the isolated outer coastline and facilities dotted across the continent's interior. Several small lakes and steep mountain outcrops, break up the terrain in the interior and limit approaches to certain facilities. Ogma Bio Laboratory stands out in this regard; it's sheltered on three sides by mountains!

There are lots of trees on this continent, and lots of cover in general. Land vehicles are feasible, but only in certain areas; driving into particularly rough parts of the continent's interior is not advised.

This continent provides great scope for sneak attacks and hidden forces. Be alert, and use the terrain to your advantage.

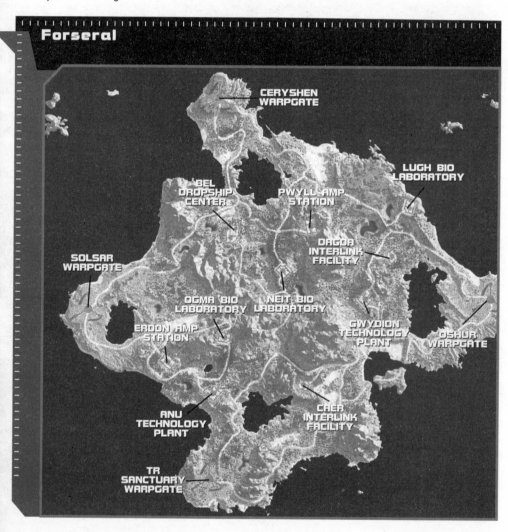

HOSSIN

Hossin is a lush, tropical continent complete with swamps. It's essentially two smaller continents, split down the middle by water. The western part is larger and contains more facilities, but the eastern part contains two Warp Gates and a DropShip Center. A central island hosts an Interlink Facility and is a logical staging point for forays to either side.

While the terrain isn't as rough as on many other continents, the lush cover and swamps provide ample opportunities to hide personnel or vehicles. Both land and air vehicles are valuable here, though land vehicles crossing the central island have to traverse multiple bridges—a dangerous proposition if the enemy is alert.

Hossin

CHAC TECHNOLOGY PLANT

KISIN INTERLINK FACILITY

CERYSHEN WARPGATE

SOLSAR WARPGATE

CHANDON TECHNOLOGY PLANT

ACAN BIO LABORATORY

NAUNI DROPSHIP CENTER

IXTAB AMP STATION

VOLTAN INTERLINK FACILITY

ZOTZ BIO LABORATORY

HURAKAN INTERLINK FACILITY

OSHU WARPGATE

MULAG TECHNOLOGY PLANT

BITEL BIO LABORATORY

VS SANCTUARY WARPGATE

ISHUNDAR

Ishundar is large, arid, bleak, and comparatively featureless save for a few small saltwater lakes. The terrain is rough, but most of the hills are navigable, so land vehicles can pick and choose their own routes, often avoiding roads in the process.

A large canyon in the continent's center is the exception to this rule; it forces vehicles into a few well-defined paths.

If you love wide-open warfare, and you hate having to constantly check the map for mountains, rivers, and other substantial landscape features, Ishundar will appeal to you. Similarly, if you like terrain that favors land vehicles, this is the place for you.

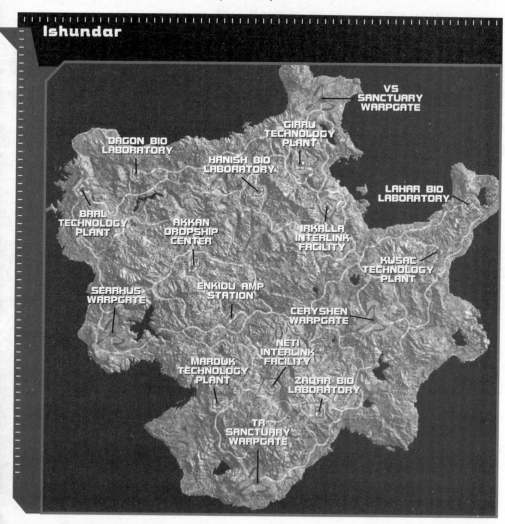

OSHUR

Oshur is somewhat like Ishundar: arid, with choppy terrain, but not much in the way of mountains. There's a fairly even distribution of facilities across the continent.

A key here is to use the terrain to conceal your forces. The lack of huge cliffs or tall hills might make it seem that ambush is impossible, but, in fact, you can move with relative stealth if you stick to the valleys.

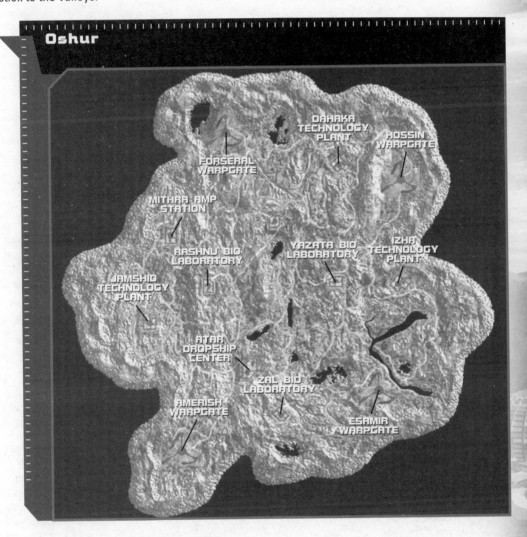

Oshur

- DAHAKA TECHNOLOGY PLANT
- HOSSIN WARPGATE
- FORSERAL WARPGATE
- MITHRA AMP STATION
- YAZATA BIO LABORATORY
- IZHA TECHNOLOGY PLANT
- RASHNU BIO LABORATORY
- JAMSHID TECHNOLOGY PLANT
- ATAR DROPSHIP CENTER
- ZAL BIO LABORATORY
- AMERISH WARPGATE
- ESAMIR WARPGATE

SEARHUS

A massive crater dominates the interior of this continent. Three facilities nestle inside the crater, several dot the flat ground outside it, and a few are scattered along its slopes.

Controlling one of the interior facilities gives you a good shot at taking over the others. The ridge facilities are in stronger positions; they control the high ground, and while they're fairly isolated, they're also quite defensible.

The perimeter facilities are easy to travel to, thanks to the flat coastal terrain with its continent-circling network of roads. They're also quite scattered and isolated, so holding one facility doesn't entitle you to easy attacks on any other facility.

Ground-vehicle specialists will prefer fighting for control of the outer facilities, where the terrain is (comparatively) smooth and forgiving. The slopes and the interior are better suited to aircraft and infantry.

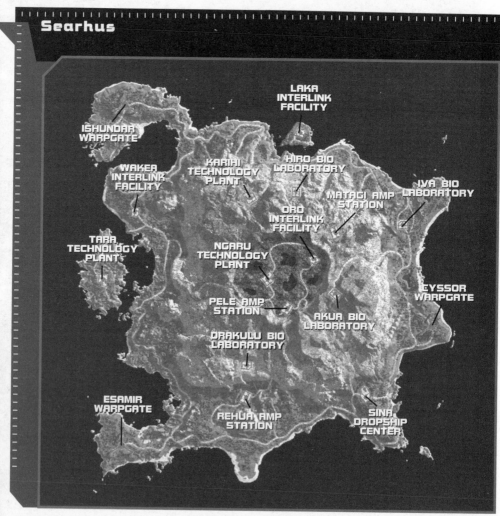

Searhus

LAKA INTERLINK FACILITY

ISHUNDAR WARPGATE

WAKER INTERLINK FACILITY

KARIHI TECHNOLOGY PLANT

HIRO BIO LABORATORY

MATAGI AMP STATION

IVA BIO LABORATORY

ORO INTERLINK FACILITY

TARA TECHNOLOGY PLANT

NGARU TECHNOLOGY PLANT

CYSSOR WARPGATE

PELE AMP STATION

AKUA BIO LABORATORY

DRAKULU BIO LABORATORY

ESAMIR WARPGATE

REHUA AMP STATION

SINA DROPSHIP CENTER

SOLSAR

Solsar features desert terrain, but unlike the other desert continents, Solsar has lots of impassable cliffs. Off-road opportunities are rare, so vehicles are usually forced to take predictable paths. A large oasis (read: lake) keeps players out of the continent's center.

Facilities are scattered and relatively easy to defend, thanks to the deep canyons and tall cliffs that limit attackers' approaches. This continent is a defense-minded player's dream.

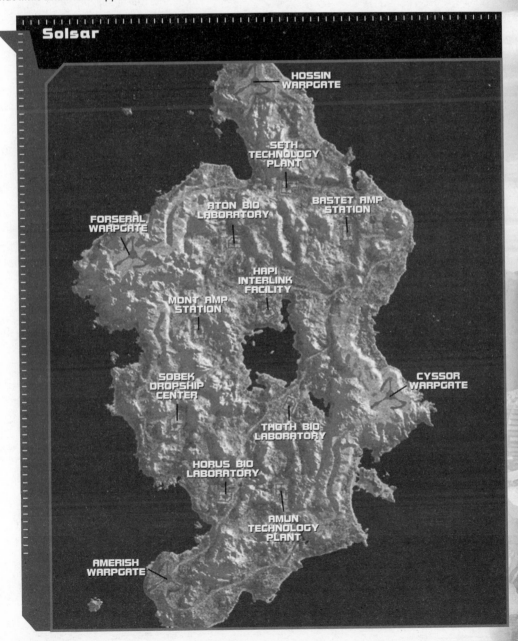

Solsar

- HOSSIN WARPGATE
- SETH TECHNOLOGY PLANT
- BASTET AMP STATION
- ATON BIO LABORATORY
- FORSERAL WARPGATE
- HAPI INTERLINK FACILITY
- MONT AMP STATION
- SOBEK DROPSHIP CENTER
- CYSSOR WARPGATE
- THOTH BIO LABORATORY
- HORUS BIO LABORATORY
- AMUN TECHNOLOGY PLANT
- AMERISH WARPGATE

FACILITIES (A.K.A. BASES)

Facilities, also known as bases or installations, are the key to controlling Auraxis™. Your Empire's goal is to control as many facilities as possible.

All facilities provide certain basic resources, such as Equipment Terminals and Medical Terminals. They're all powered by Generators, and they all have Command Consoles, which may be hacked to transfer power from one Empire to another.

Facilities also have Matrix Panels that you can bind to, and a room full of Respawn Tubes. They typically have a Vehicle Terminal (usually outdoors, in the courtyard), though the vehicles you can purchase vary from one facility to the next.

Some facilities provide extra services; Bio Labs have Implant Terminals and Certification Terminals, for example.

Finally, some facility types provide benefits that extend to other continental facilities. These benefits are provided to all facilities connected via the Continental Lattice.

A NOTE ON FACILITIES AND ANTS

Facilities are powered by NTUs (Nanite Technology Units), which are stored in a silo in the facility's courtyard. An indicator on the silo lets you see how much power remains. (You can also get that information from the Tactical View of your map.)

NTUs are consumed when players respawn inside the facility. This is the main NTU drain on most facilities.

Facilities are capable of auto-repairing broken elements such as Equipment Terminals and Generators. Facilities will begin the auto-repair process soon after an element is damaged. The element does not need to be destroyed before the auto-repair process will attempt to fix it. If a terminal has 499 out of 500 armor points, the auto-repair function of the facility will attempt to repair that one missing armor point thus consuming a tiny bit of NTU. However, if the auto-repair function repairs back 250 armor points, then much more NTU will be consumed.

NOTE

If you infiltrate a facility well behind enemy lines, and that facility is low on NTUs, one strategy is to break lots of equipment and wait for it to auto-repair. The repair process might eat up the base's remaining NTUs, and cause it to turn neutral. Since you can *always* capture a neutral base, even if you don't possess any adjacent bases, this is an effective way of circumventing the Continental Lattice.

AMP STATIONS

All vehicles have shield capacity. Vehicles' shields are charged up by driving the vehicle into the Sphere of Influence of an Amp Station, or the SOI of a facility *connected to* an Amp Station via the Continental Lattice.

If you purchase a vehicle at a facility that's isolated from the Continental Lattice (and that is not an Amp Station), therefore, your vehicle will not start out with any shield power. You'll need to drive the vehicle into the SOI of an Amp Station (or a connected facility) to make those shields power up.

VEHICLES

Amp Stations' outdoor Vehicle Terminals are initially limited to light vehicles. You can create:

- Utility vehicles (AMS and ANT)
- Four-wheelers (Assault Basilisk, Wraith)
- Mosquito
- Lightning
- Harasser
- Deliverer

However, this changes if you also possess a Tech Plant on the same continent. With the Tech Plant, you may also create heavy assault vehicles, including:

- Assault buggies (Thresher, Marauder, Enforcer)
- Assault tanks (MagRider, Prowler, Vanguard)
- Reaver
- Sunderer

The only thing an Amp Station can never produce is a Galaxy. Only a DropShip Center (or a Sanctuary) can produce those.

FLOOR PLAN

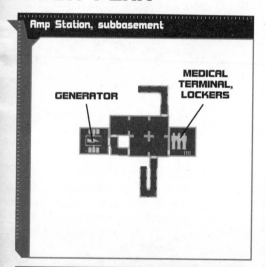

Amp Station, subbasement

GENERATOR

MEDICAL TERMINAL, LOCKERS

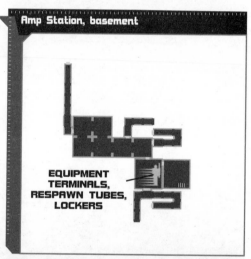

Amp Station, basement

EQUIPMENT TERMINALS, RESPAWN TUBES, LOCKERS

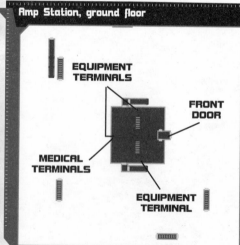

Amp Station, ground floor

EQUIPMENT TERMINALS

FRONT DOOR

MEDICAL TERMINALS

EQUIPMENT TERMINAL

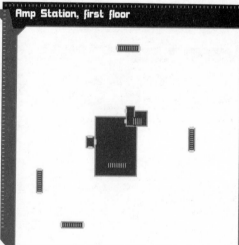

Amp Station, first floor

Amp Station, second floor

CONTROL
TERMINAL

Amp Stations feature a Command Console on the top floor, accessible from both the interior stairs and exterior walkways. Upstairs Command Consoles are more exposed than basement Consoles, but on the plus side, some defenders can stand outside, effectively defending both the base's courtyard and the Console simultaneously.

Equipment Terminals and Respawn Tubes are in the basement, while the Generator is in the subbasement. Since the Command Console and Generator are quite far apart, and since most defenders will pack into the upper floors, attacking the subbasement Generator is not usually a difficult task.

BIO LABS

Every time a character is killed, it takes a certain amount of time for that character to respawn. Bio Labs decrease the amount of time friendly units take to respawn, both inside the Bio Lab's SOI, and inside the SOI of friendly facilities connected to the Bio Lab via the Continental Lattice.

The end result is a more efficient fighting force, which spends more time fighting and less time waiting to respawn. This can have a profound effect on your Empire's effectiveness.

Bio Labs contain Implant Terminals and Certification Terminals; no other facilities outside of a Sanctuary contain these.

VEHICLES

Bio Labs' vehicle creation capabilities are identical to those of the Amp Station. If you don't control a Tech Plant on the continent, the Bio Lab is limited to producing lightly armed and armored vehicles. With the addition of a Tech Plant, everything short of a Galaxy may be created at the Bio Lab.

Refer to the Amp Station section for a complete list of vehicles that can be produced.

FLOOR PLAN

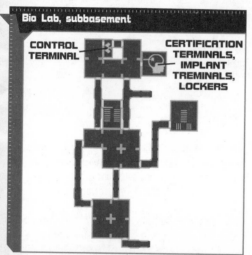

Bio Lab, subbasement

CONTROL TERMINAL

CERTIFICATION TERMINALS, IMPLANT TREMINALS, LOCKERS

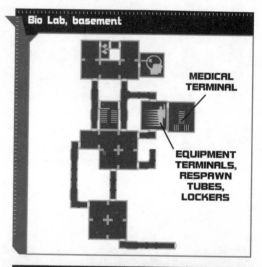

Bio Lab, basement

MEDICAL TERMINAL

EQUIPMENT TERMINALS, RESPAWN TUBES, LOCKERS

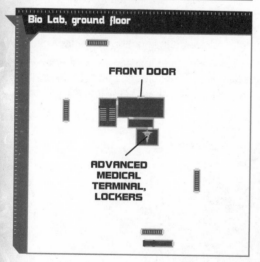

Bio Lab, ground floor

FRONT DOOR

ADVANCED MEDICAL TERMINAL, LOCKERS

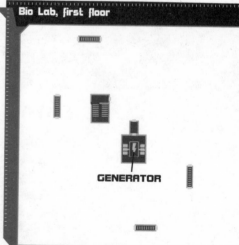

Bio Lab, first floor

GENERATOR

The Bio Lab's Command Console is tucked safely in the subbasement. The two halls leading to the Command Console area are parallel, and they're easy for defenders to monitor; this is a tough place to assault.

Respawn Tubes and Equipment Terminals are packed into the basement level.

There's an Advanced Medical Terminal on the ground floor, which is handy for defenders who want to pop in for quick healing, then get back outside.

The Generator is in its own little room on the top floor, accessible only from the outside. This makes it very difficult to defend, counterbalancing the relatively secure Command Console location.

If an attack on a Bio Lab is going badly, it's usually not too difficult to get up to the roof and take down the Generator.

DROPSHIP CENTERS

DropShip Centers are the only non-Sanctuary facilities where you can create the Galaxy transport. The Galaxy is the best way of moving a large group across a continent; it holds lots of infantry, can fly over any terrain obstacle, has excellent armor and decent weaponry, and even allows the transport of certain vehicles. As a result, DropShip Centers are quite valuable as staging areas for raids on other facilities.

DropShip Centers have vehicle pads that repair and re-arm any vehicle parked on them. Drive your vehicle onto one of these pads, and watch as the vehicle's armor and ammo are both replenished.

VEHICLES

In addition to the Galaxy, the DropShip Center may create light vehicles (just like an Amp Station). With the addition of a Tech Plant on the same continent, it has access to heavy vehicles, too.

Refer to the Amp Station lists for details on which vehicles are available with or without a Tech Center. Just remember that DropShip Centers can always create a Galaxy, in addition to the other vehicles.

NOTE

If you control a Tech Plant on the same continent, a DropShip Center is the only place (outside of your Sanctuary) where you may create *all* vehicles in the game.

FLOOR PLAN

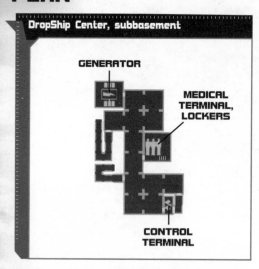

DropShip Center, subbasement

GENERATOR

MEDICAL TERMINAL, LOCKERS

CONTROL TERMINAL

DropShip Center, basement

EQUIPMENT TERMINALS, RESPAWN TUBES, LOCKERS

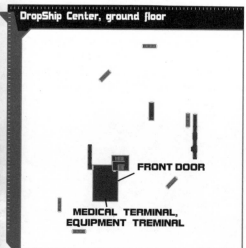

DropShip Center, ground floor

FRONT DOOR

MEDICAL TERMINAL, EQUIPMENT TREMINAL

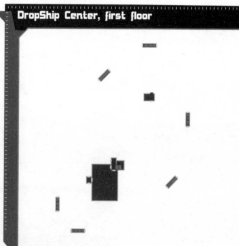

DropShip Center, first floor

DropShip Centers are hard to assault. They pack the Command Console and Generator into the subbasement, with the Respawn Tubes and Equipment Terminals in the basement nearby. The upper floors are largely devoid of important gear.

When attacking a well-defended DropShip Center, be sure to bring overwhelming numbers. A good plan is to completely destroy the exterior defenders and take over the outside of the base. Park an AMS nearby. Then, get inside and assault the lower levels in waves. Destroying the Equipment Terminals or Respawn Tubes can greatly help your assault.

INTERLINK FACILITIES

Interlink Facilities place enemy vehicles within their SOI (and within connected facilities' SOI) on your allies' Proximity Maps. The ability to see enemy vehicles on the Proximity Map is a very useful tool.

Interlink Facilities also upgrade linked facilities' unmanned Wall Turrets. Those turrets will fire at enemy vehicles when connected to an Interlink Facility via the Continental Lattice.

NOTE

are stealthy vehicles. They won't automatically show up on maps, or automatically be fired at by turrets—regardless of whether an Interlink Facility is involved.

VEHICLES

Like the Amp Station and Bio Lab, if no continental Tech Plant is controlled Interlink Facilities may create only light vehicles.

With the addition of a Tech Plant, an Interlink Facility may create all vehicles, save for the Galaxy. Refer to the Amp Station entry for a full vehicle list.

FLOOR PLAN

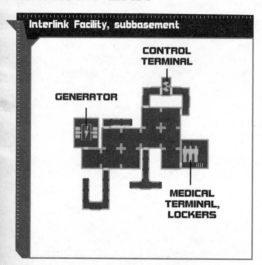

Interlink Facility, subbasement

CONTROL TERMINAL

GENERATOR

MEDICAL TERMINAL, LOCKERS

Interlink Facility, basement

EQUIPMENT TERMINALS, RESPAWN TUBES, LOCKERS

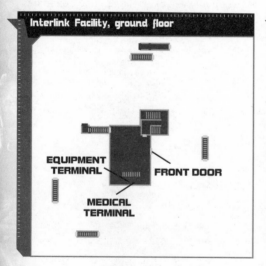

Interlink Facility, ground floor

EQUIPMENT TERMINAL

FRONT DOOR

MEDICAL TERMINAL

Interlink Facility, first floor

Interlink Facility, second floor

Like the DropShip Center, the Interlink Facility packs most of its critical gear into the lower floors. This makes it tough to assault.

The Command Console and Generator are in the subbasement; the Respawn Tubes and Equipment Terminals are just upstairs, in the basement. The upper floors are largely devoid of gear.

As with the DropShip Center, well-guarded Interlink Facilities are very tough to assault.

TECH PLANTS

If you've been paying attention to the last few sections, you already know what Tech Plants do. They augment the vehicle-creation abilities of friendly facilities that would otherwise be able to create only light combat (or non-combat) vehicles.

Specifically, if you control a Tech Plant on a particular continent, all friendly facilities connected via the Continental Lattice become capable of producing all vehicle types short of the Galaxy.

VEHICLES

As you might expect, Tech Plants can create any vehicle except the Galaxy. This makes them useful staging points for large, vehicle-based assaults.

FLOOR PLAN

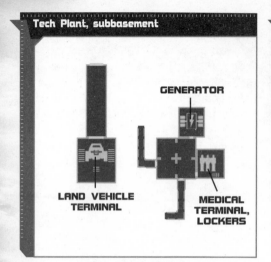

Tech Plant, subbasement

GENERATOR

LAND VEHICLE TERMINAL

MEDICAL TERMINAL, LOCKERS

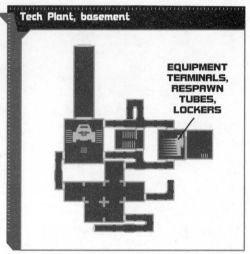

Tech Plant, basement

EQUIPMENT TERMINALS, RESPAWN TUBES, LOCKERS

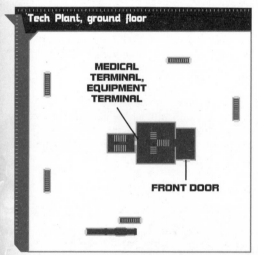

Tech Plant, ground floor

MEDICAL TERMINAL, EQUIPMENT TERMINAL

FRONT DOOR

Tech Plant, first floor

AIR VEHICLE TERMINAL

CONTROL TERMINAL

Tech Plants have an unusual layout. The Generator shares room in the subbasement with the underground Vehicle Terminal, which produces only land vehicles. Respawn Tubes and Equipment Terminals are in the basement.

The top floor holds both the Command Console and a special Vehicle Terminal for air vehicles.

The indoor Vehicle Terminals are somewhat less likely to be hacked or destroyed than outdoor terminals. The separation into land and air terminals allows the production of more vehicles, faster.

Because of their floor layout and Command Console placement, Tech Plants aren't particularly tough to assault, but be assured that a well-defended Tech Plant will field lots of heavy combat vehicles.

TOWERS

Facilities and Towers are the two controllable structure types on any Battle Continent. A typical facility is flanked by several Towers, which are usually named after the facility itself, the Tower type, and the Tower's direction from the facility. (For example, a Gun Tower south of the Kaang facility would be called the South Kaang Gun Tower.)

There are three Tower types: Watch Towers, Gun Towers, and Air Towers. Air Towers have Wall Turrets and a landing pad; Gun Towers have Wall Turrets but no landing pad; and Watch Towers have neither.

Towers contain Respawn Tubes, Equipment Terminals, a Command Console, and Lockers in a basement level. They're effectively mini-bases, and they're extremely valuable for any base assault. While they don't have the mobility and unpredictability of an AMS, they cannot be destroyed, and Gun Towers and Air Towers have useful defenses as well.

Take control of at least one Tower before launching an assault on an opponent's base. Even if you already have an AMS, the Tower provides an excellent alternative for respawning players—plus, it allows you to suit up in MAXes, while an AMS does not.

TRANSPORTATION

There are various methods of getting around in *PlanetSide*. Running and driving a vehicle are the obvious forms for relatively short-distance travel, but let's take a quick look at some useful techniques for traveling long distances.

WARP GATES

Warp Gates allow you to move vehicles from one continent to another. Unlike the HART Shuttle, they're always available, without a wait.

If your Empire possesses vehicle-building facilities on a particular continent, you don't need to use Warp Gates; you can create vehicles at those facilities instead. However, in cases where the facilities can't produce the vehicles you want, or where the Warp Gate is actually closer to your target than your nearest base, create the vehicle in your Sanctuary (or on a different continent) and drive through the Warp Gate to your destination.

Also, use the Warp Gate if the HART Shuttle isn't taking off for a while and if it's only one Gate hop to your destination. If you need to pass through more than one Gate and you don't have a relatively speedy vehicle, you might as well wait for the Shuttle.

Warp Gates connected to a Sanctuary or a locked continent are "aligned" to a particular Empire and show up as that empire's color on the Tactical View. Enemies cannot go inside the protective sphere of these Warp Gates. All other Warp Gates are neutral (shown on the map by a yellow Sphere of Influence), and anyone can go inside. However, no weapons may be used inside the Warp Gate's SOI.

Warp Gates are also necessary for charging up ANTs. Drive an ANT into a friendly or neutral Warp Gate's Sphere of Influence and deploy it to charge it up.

NOTE

You cannot physically get inside an enemy Warp Gate's Sphere of Influence. The SOI perimeter acts like a wall to members of other Empires.

HART (HIGH ALTITUDE RAPID TRANSPORT) SHUTTLE

Each Sanctuary has two HART Shuttle buildings. HART Shuttles leave these buildings at designated intervals.

Even if it's a long wait, the Shuttle is often the best way of traveling—if you don't have a vehicle (or a ride on someone else's vehicle). It can drop you more or less where you want to go.

If it's a long wait and the destination is only one Warp Gate hop away, use the Warp Gates instead—especially if you have a vehicle.

DECONSTRUCTION

You can enter a Respawn Tube, in either a facility or an AMS, and deconstruct your character. Then you can instantly reappear in any valid spot where you'd normally be allowed to respawn. The difference between this and getting killed is that you get to keep your armor and gear.

This technique is effective if you respawn and then decide that you want to be somewhere else instead. Note that deconstruction won't be very useful unless you make a habit of manually binding to Matrix Panels at each friendly facility and AMS, since your respawn options will otherwise be limited to the nearest facilities, Towers, and AMS locations.

You can deconstruct a MAX at an AMS and reappear in a facility, but you can never reconstruct a MAX at an AMS.

RECALL TO SANCTUARY

Let's say you're stuck halfway across the continent from your current target, and you decide you'd rather be on a completely different continent anyway. In this case it may be faster to Recall to Sanctuary, and from there take the HART Shuttle to a point much closer to your target, than to get there using Warp Gates.

Having a whole squad Recall to Sanctuary is also a useful way to get everyone together, especially when your plans have fallen apart and everyone is scattered. From there, it's easy to grab a few vehicles and use a Warp Gate to re-enter the battlefield.

INSTANT ACTION

If you're all geared up and itching for a fight, and you aren't very picky about where you want to go, press esc and select Instant Action. You'll be immediately transported somewhere with some fighting going on.

This option works best if you don't have a squad yet. You can look for one when you reach your destination. If you do have a squad, this is a bad idea. Instant Action puts you somewhere random, so you risk splitting up the squad if you choose it.

PLANET-WIDE GAME SYSTEMS

We conclude this chapter with a look at two systems that affect the entire planet: the Empire Balancing System and the Grief System.

EMPIRE BALANCE

PlanetSide features three warring Empires. What happens if a disproportionate number of players decide to play for one Empire and crush the other two?

A running total is kept of the number of hours logged by players from each Empire. Those numbers are expressed as a percentage of hours played by each Empire. For example: During the last 24 hours on a particular server, the following hours were logged by players:

New Conglomerate: 4,500 hours

Terran Republic: 3,000 hours

Vanu Sovereignty: 2,500 hours

This breaks down to the following percentages:

New Conglomerate: 45 percent

Terran Republic: 30 percent

Vanu Sovereignty: 25 percent

These percentages are compared against the target percentage (which is 33 percent for all three Empires) by subtracting 33 percent from the actual percentages. Hence:

New Conglomerate: 45 percent - 33 percent = 12 percent over target percentage

Terran Republic: 30 percent - 33 percent = 3 percent under target percentage

Vanu Sovereignty: 25 percent - 33 percent = 8 percent under target percentage

Experience point and hit point bonuses and penalties are now applied.

EXPERIENCE POINT BONUSES AND PENALTIES

Experience point bonuses and penalties are based directly on each Empire's playing time surplus or deficit.

In our example, the New Conglomerate is 12 percent over the target mark, so New Conglomerate players will all earn 12 percent fewer BEPs and CEPs than they otherwise would.

Meanwhile, Terran Republic players will earn 3 percent more BEPs and CEPs than usual, and Vanu Sovereignty players will earn 8 percent more BEPs and CEPs.

This situation will persist until the teams become more balanced.

HIT POINT (HEALTH) PENALTIES

When Empires are logging more than 5 percent over the target percentage, hit point penalties start to occur.

The formula for hit point penalties is to take the play time surplus and subtract 5 percent. Then, for every 2 percent of surplus that still remains (rounded down), players for that Empire have one hit point subtracted from their maximum total.

In our example, the New Conglomerate is 12 percent over the target mark. Subtract 5 percent and you're left with 7 percent. Divide 7 percent by 2 to get 3.5, and round down to 3. Players for the New Conglomerate will have 3 hit points subtracted from their maximums.

Again, this situation persists until the play balance evens out. The evening process is slow and gradual.

GRIEF SYSTEM

The Grief System is in place to prevent players from turning on their allies and ruining the game for everyone.

Whenever you do damage to a friendly player, vehicle, or object, you accumulate Grief Points. (Grief Points are also awarded when you shoot objects affiliated with a friendly base, such as Generators and Equipment Terminals.)

If you accumulate enough Grief Points, you'll start to gain Grief Levels. At the first level you're simply warned. At higher levels your ability to use weapons and items will be temporarily removed. At the highest levels you'll be banned from the game for a few days.

Grief Points dissipate automatically over time, so you don't have to worry if you're careful and well-intentioned.

NOTE

Note that Grief Points dissipate over game time, not real time. You can't just log off and then log back in later, expecting to find all your Grief Points gone.

You don't accumulate Grief Points for hurting fellow squad members. That's because the developers understand that friendly fire sometimes happens, despite your best intentions.

NOTE

If someone on your squad is intentionally causing problems, kick him or her off immediately. That way, the troublemaker will start accumulating Grief Points if he or she keeps it up.

If you accumulate extremely high Grief Points, play it safe for a while as they dissipate. Don't use weapons with serious splash damage, don't shoot at anyone before you're absolutely sure of their Empire (you should always do this anyway!), and don't fire into crowds. Also, be extra-careful when driving a vehicle, as mowing down your teammates is definitely a bad idea.

CHAPTER 7: CERTIFICATIONS, IMPLANTS, AND CHARACTER DEVELOPMENT

PlanetSide encourages cooperation in various ways; one such way is by limiting each character's skills and abilities. Nobody—not even the highest-level character—can learn *every* Certification. In fact, it's impossible to even get close. That's one of many good reasons to form a squad: You get the benefit of everyone's combined Certifications and skills.

Base your character decisions on the sort of game you like to play. If you like stealth, load up on Certifications like Infiltration Suit, Hacking, and Wraith. If you want to blow up heavily armored targets, Anti-Vehicle Weapons Certification is for you. This chapter doesn't tell you what Certifications and Implants to get; rather, it informs you about the process of developing a character and presents options so you can make your own informed decision.

OVERVIEW OF CHARACTER PLANNING

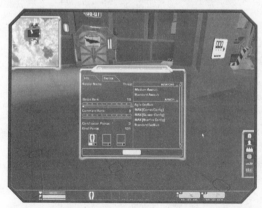

Most characters gain Battle Experience Points (BEPs) through combat and base capture. (Squad leaders gain Command Experience Points in some circumstances, instead; more on that later.) Gain enough BEPs, and the character rises in Battle Rank.

Each Battle Rank brings more Certification Points, which may be spent on Certifications. Also, at certain Battle Ranks the character gains Implant Slots. Characters with free Implant Slots can have performance-enhancing cybernetic devices installed at an Implant Terminal.

Fortunately, no character-related decision in *PlanetSide* is permanent. Implants can be removed, clearing the way for different Implants; similarly, Certifications can be unlearned, freeing up your Certification Points for different skills.

There is, however, a 24-hour "Certification Point Lock." You must wait 24 hours after unlearning multiple Certifications before most of the Certification Points become free to spend on a new Certification. Since changes cannot be made instantly, it's worthwhile to put a little thought into your decisions.

MULTIPLE CHARACTERS

There are several good reasons to have more than one character in *PlanetSide*. The game allows you to have up to four distinct characters, but that they must all belong to the same Empire.

No character can have a complete skill set, and it's no fun spending 24 hours while you clear away old Certifications, waiting for the points to pick new ones. Add in the fact that it's easy to gain a few quick Battle Ranks, and you'll see why it's useful to have an extra character or two.

Your extra character(s) can have very different skill sets. While your primary character may be an engineer/fighter, your secondary character might be a stealth hacker. A third character could be a vehicle specialist.

Even when you decide to rearrange your primary character's skills, it's nice to have backups. You can play them during the awkward transition periods when your primary character's Certification Points are inaccessible.

BEPS AND BATTLE RANK

You know that BEPs are necessary to gain Battle Rank. You know that each new Battle Rank provides certain benefits. But exactly how many BEPs do you need, and what benefits are provided? The following table explains everything:

BATTLE RANKS AND BENEFITS

Battle Rank	Required BEPs	Benefits
1	0	—
2	1,000	1 Certification Point
3	3,000	1 Certification Point
4	7,500	1 Certification Point
5	15,000	1 Certification Point
6	30,000	1 Certification Point, 1 Implant Slot, Uniform Change
7	45,000	1 Certification Point
8	67,500	1 Certification Point
9	101,250	1 Certification Point
10	126,563	1 Certification Point
11	158,203	1 Certification Point
12	197,754	1 Certification Point, 1 Implant Slot, Uniform Change
13	247,192	1 Certification Point
14	308,990	1 Certification Point
15	386,238	1 Certification Point
16	482,798	1 Certification Point
17	603,497	1 Certification Point
18	754,371	1 Certification Point, 1 Implant Slot, Uniform Change
19	942,964	1 Certification Point
20	1,178,705	1 Certification Point

BATTLE RANK BREAKDOWN

As you can see from the table, early Battle Ranks come easily. It's much tougher to reach the higher levels and garner all the associated benefits.

The Uniform Change mentioned at Battle Ranks 6, 12, and 18 refers to slight changes to your character's uniform color. These changes don't provide any extra protection, but they do let everyone know that you've attained a certain rank.

As the table shows, no character in *PlanetSide*—no matter how experienced—can do everything. A character has a maximum of 23 Certification Points (four at Level 1, and then an additional point for each level thereafter) and three Implant Slots.

We consider Battle Rank 12 a "sweet spot," because it doesn't require a tremendous number of BEPs to get there, but at that level, your character has two Implant Slots and enough Certification Points to be very good in a particular area. You might even be able to fit in a side specialization.

GAINING EXPERIENCE

BEPs are gained by killing enemies, capturing bases, and refueling bases.

The exact amount of experience provided by any particular action varies based on a formula too complex to delve into. For example, base captures earn variable experience based on the amount of resistance (enemy soldiers and vehicles) in the area.

Kills provide experience based on the target's armor, the weapon in the target's hand when you score the kill, and how long the target was alive. Heavier-armored targets provide more BEPs, as do targets with bigger guns in their hands. Newly respawned players are worth zero BEPs, to discourage cheap kills at enemy Respawn Tubes or AMSes—but as time passes they become more valuable. A character who's been in the game for five minutes without dying will reach his or her maximum point value.

When you destroy vehicles with players inside, the BEP values of the passengers are multiplied by a "vehicle multiplier." For example, a character currently worth 70 BEPs might be in a tank with a 5x multiplier. Destroy the tank, and you collect 350 BEPs.

NOTE

Again, we stress that the actual BEP numbers awarded for kills are likely to be tweaked and re-tweaked over time. But now that you understand the factors that go into calculating BEPs, you'll be able to figure out the relative scales, based on how many BEPs you're awarded for killing various characters.

CERTIFICATIONS

Certifications enable your character to use various weapons, vehicles, and inventory items. Since we've already discussed those weapons, vehicles, and items in previous chapters, this chapter focuses mainly on the Certifications themselves—specifically, the Certification Point costs and their relative value for different character types.

WEAPON CERTIFICATIONS

The following Certifications allow your character to use particular weapons.

It's tempting for new players to load up on weapon Certifications and neglect other areas. This is not recommended, for two reasons. First, you'll find that without good armor and good supplemental skills, there's a limit to what you can achieve. Second, it's those "other" skills that make you most appealing to a squad.

STANDARD WEAPONS (CANNOT BE UNLEARNED)

Certification Point Cost: —

Prerequisites: —

Prerequisite for: Medium Assault Weapons

Allows Use of: AMP, Suppressor, Beamer (VS), Repeater (TR), Scatter Pistol (NC)

The Standard Weapons Certification is a default Certification that can't be unlearned. It allows a character to use the general pool Suppressor and AMP; it also lets you use the Beamer (Vanu Sovereignty), Repeater (Terran Republic), and Scatter-Pistol (New Conglomerate).

> ## TIP
> While you can't purchase other Empires' weapons at friendly Equipment Terminals, you *can* loot them from bodies. Bear this in mind, because with the right weapon Certification, you can use those other Empires' guns.

Let's skip the diplomacy: These are not potent weapons. They tend to have limited range, moderate accuracy, and low power. In the right circumstances, they can be deadly; spies in Infiltration Suits, for example, can usually kill anything short of a MAX by sneaking right up on someone's back and unloading one of these weapons. Several direct hits at close range will usually do the trick.

In standard combat situations, however, these weapons won't get you far. You'll need something else quickly, especially if your character is more of a fighter than a support player. Even support players will eventually want to upgrade.

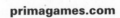

MEDIUM ASSAULT WEAPONS

Certification Point Cost: 2

Prerequisites: —

Prerequisite for: Anti-Vehicle Weapons, Heavy Assault Weapons, Special Assault Weapons, Sniping

Allows Use of: Sweeper, Punisher, Pulsar (VS), Repeater (TR), Gauss Rifle (NC)

Since Medium Assault Weapons Certification is a prerequisite for most other weapon Certifications, and since even players focusing on non-combat tasks eventually want better guns, almost every character will learn this Certification sooner rather than later.

This is a versatile class of weapons. The Sweeper and Punisher alone are quite capable, the Punisher being a general-purpose assault rifle and the Sweeper being a good close-range weapon. The Empire-specific weapons are just bonuses.

Any character whose main focus is infantry combat needs this skill immediately. Other characters should take it when it becomes convenient; many of them won't need any weapons Certifications besides this.

HEAVY ASSAULT WEAPONS

Certification Point Cost: 4

Prerequisites: Medium Assault Weapons

Prerequisite for: —

Allows Use of: Lasher (VS), Mini-Chaingun (TR), Jackhammer (NC)

Characters with Heavy Assault Weapons Certification can use the Lasher, Mini-Chaingun, and Jackhammer. These weapons represent the pinnacle of anti-personnel weaponry. Non-MAX armor types cannot carry anything better than this for close-range combat vs. opponents in typical (non-MAX) armor.

If your character is a serious anti-personnel fighter, this Certification may be necessary. However, always bear in mind that MAXes have their own built-in weapons. If you want to be a heavily armed and armored behemoth, perhaps you want to go the MAX route instead.

Also bear in mind that some of the medium assault weapons are actually better than these weapons in medium- to long-range combat. If you prefer weapons with range and versatility, you might not need this Certification.

Combat specialists will want this Certification so they can really mow through infantry.

ANTI-VEHICULAR WEAPONS

Certification Point Cost: 3

Prerequisites: Medium Assault Weapons

Prerequisite for: —

Allows Use of: Lancer (VS), Striker (TR), Phoenix (NC)

Anti-vehicular weaponry includes the Empire-specific Lancer, Striker, and Phoenix. These weapons all deal massive damage to vehicles and MAXes, but are surprisingly weak against lesser armor types. These weapons' ammo is big and bulky, so you wouldn't want to waste it on infantry anyway.

Anti-vehicular weapons are fairly easy to overlook. Most of your foes are on foot, after all. But MAXes are vulnerable to these weapons, and consider how much of an impact enemy vehicles can have on the game.

The bottom line is that these weapons are strongly recommended for anyone playing a serious combat role.

SNIPING

Certification Point Cost: 3

Prerequisites: Medium Assault Weapons

Prerequisite for: —

Allows Use of: Bolt Driver

Snipers carry the Bolt Driver sniper rifle. Sniping can be tactically useful in certain situations, but there are limits. That's why, for most team-oriented players, the Sniping Certification is not a high priority.

If you do grab this Certification, try sniping right away and see if it's for you. Sniping is a specialized sort of fighting, and it's hard to snipe while trying to accomplish other goals; generally, if you're sniping, the sniping *is* your goal.

If you love sniping, keep the Certification; if not, don't be afraid to cash it in. This is just one of those Certifications that you either use, or you don't. There's not much middle ground.

SPECIAL ASSAULT WEAPONS

Certification Point Cost: 3

Prerequisites: Medium Assault Weapons

Prerequisite for: —

Allows Use of: Decimator, Rocklet Gun, Thumper

The Special Assault Weapons Certification allows use of three common weapons: the Decimator, Rocklet Gun, and Thumper. These weapons all fire explosive projectiles, all deal very good damage, and all have limited clip sizes. Think of them as "wildcard" weapons: extremely potent, somewhat short on ammo, and effective over the short haul. Any squad can benefit from having a member with some of these weapons.

ARMOR CERTIFICATIONS

Armor Certifications determine more than anything else what your character can do. Inventory size, ability to use particular weapons and tools, and ability to pilot or ride in different vehicles is all tied to the armor your character is wearing.

STANDARD EXOSUIT (CANNOT BE UNLEARNED)

Certification Point Cost: —

Prerequisites: —

Prerequisite for: —

Allows Use of: Standard Exosuit

This standard Certification is issued to every player and cannot be unlearned. New players and newly respawned players always start out in Standard Exosuits (which is, effectively, no armor at all). They can and should get to an Inventory Terminal as quickly as possible and grab an Agile Exosuit.

To put it bluntly: There's seldom any reason to stick with the Standard Exosuit when you have access to an Equipment Terminal. The Agile Exosuit is an upgrade.

AGILE EXOSUIT (CANNOT BE UNLEARNED)

Certification Point Cost: —

Prerequisites: —

Prerequisite for: —

Allows Use of: Agile Exosuit

This standard Certification is issued to every player and cannot be unlearned. Agile Exosuits offer minimal protection but good speed and reasonable inventory capacity. They're superior to Standard Exosuits, but slower.

Agile Exosuits are the most vulnerable of the legitimate combat armors, but they're a good choice for snipers, drivers, and anyone who likes mobility. Some tasks (such as piloting most vehicles) cannot be performed in heavier armor.

Also, some players prefer the Agile Exosuit to Reinforced Battle Armor, simply because of its superior speed. It all depends on your preferences and combat style.

REINFORCED EXOSUIT

Certification Point Cost: 3

Prerequisites: —

Prerequisite for: —

Allows Use of: Reinforced Body Armor

Reinforced Body Armor is the armor for versatile but combat-oriented characters. Pure fighting specialists can take MAXes; stealthy types will go for the Infiltration Suit. Grab the Reinforced Body Armor instead, if you plan to slug it out but also perform also useful tasks like driving, hacking, healing, or repairing things.

This Certification is a must-have for serious fighters.

ANTI-AIRCRAFT MAX

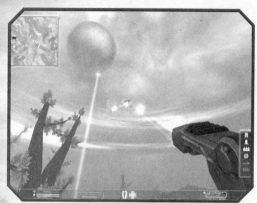

Certification Point Cost: 2

Prerequisites: —

Prerequisite for: —

Allows Use of: Starfire (VS), Burster (TR), Sparrow (NC)

The anti-aircraft MAX is the most specialized (and therefore, rare) MAX. This MAX can be very useful when defending a base, because air vehicles are a major threat. It's a lot less useful indoors, so stay outside when wearing this armor.

Pick this Certification if you love base defense and taking down aircraft. You'll wreak havoc on Mosquitoes, Reavers, and even Galaxies when you pick this Certification.

ANTI-PERSONNEL MAX

Certification Point Cost: 3

Prerequisites: —

Prerequisite for: —

Allows Use of: Quasar (VS), Pounder (TR), Scattercannon (NC)

This is the most common MAX Certification. Anti-personnel MAXes can chew through a wide range of infantry targets and are useful in just about any squad.

Since a MAX is a self-contained unit (it comes with armor and a weapon), learning a MAX Certification can be a cheap (in Certification Points) way of developing a versatile character. A high-level character could play a stealth hacker with a MAX Certification, sneaking around most of the time but jumping into a MAX and duking it out whenever pure combat is required.

This is probably the most "general-purpose" MAX Certification. Taking this Certification allows you to stick with a squad at all times and always be useful.

ANTI-VEHICULAR MAX

Certification Point Cost: 3

Prerequisites: —

Prerequisite for: —

Allows Use of: Comet (VS), Dual Cycler (TR), Falcon (NC)

The anti-vehicular MAX is quite versatile. It does well against other MAXes and vehicles (of course), and isn't too shabby against infantry either.

This Certification will earn you a spot in many squads. Like the anti-infantry MAX, it's valuable both indoors and out, especially when fighting other MAXes.

INFILTRATION SUIT

Certification Point Cost: 2

Prerequisites: —

Prerequisite for: —

Allows Use of: Infiltration Suit

This Certification allows use of the ultra-stealthy Infiltration Suit.

It is one of a few Certifications that will change the entire way you play the game. With the Infiltration Suit on you're fragile but extremely hard to notice; all sorts of hacking and scouting options open up while you have it. Most combat options close, however, so you're limited to ambushing lone non-MAXes, setting traps, or various other sneaky tricks.

If you love stealth and subterfuge, you *must* have this Certification. It paves the way for easier terminal hacking, carjacking, reconnaissance, stealth engineering, and other fiendishly entertaining endeavors.

VEHICLE CERTIFICATIONS

Vehicles are often the overlooked Certifications. Players understandably feel naked without good weapons and armor, so those things tend to be addressed before vehicles.

However, the ability to drive vehicles—especially vehicles with multiplayer capacity—makes you *extremely* attractive to a squad. You can spend most of your time inside a vehicle if that's what you like, so don't be afraid to take these Certifications right from the start.

AMS

Certification Point Cost: 2

Prerequisites: —

Prerequisite for: —

Allows Use of: AMS

The AMS is the linchpin of a typical base assault. Without one or two of these vehicles, attacking often isn't worth the bother; when your forces suffer losses, the fallen players respawn too far away to be useful.

An ideal squad contains at least one character with this Certification, and a second wouldn't hurt.

AMS driving is particularly great for high-level hackers. Hackers can hack an enemy Vehicle Terminal to quickly grab an AMS in enemy territory, and then deploy it nearby to help the assault. Or, they can carjack an existing enemy AMS and drive it off to a safer location.

The bottom line is that someone on your squad needs this skill.

NOTE

Hackers without the ability to drive an AMS can still carjack the vehicles, but they can't move them. This is still very useful, but the AMS isn't likely to last as long, as the enemy already knows where the AMS is.

ASSAULT BASILISK

Certification Point Cost: 3

Prerequisites: —

Prerequisite for: —

Allows Use of: Assault Basilisk

A Certification for the Assault Basilisk, a superb scout vehicle, is an excellent idea for players who like to scout and infiltrate, and maybe deal a little damage (especially to aircraft) with the Basilisk's light weaponry. But it's a questionable choice for those who'll stick with the squad most of the time. For them, a Certification in a bigger vehicle is in order.

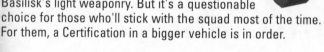

DELIVERER

Certification Point Cost: 3

Prerequisites: —

Prerequisite for: —

Allows Use of: Deliverer

The Deliverer transports lots of players from one spot to another. It's certainly not flashy, but it's very useful for moving part of a squad quickly across the landscape. It's also capable of crossing water. A Certification in this vehicle will reap dividends in a well-organized squad.

GALAXY

Certification Point Cost: 3

Prerequisites: —

Prerequisite for: —

Allows Use of: Galaxy

The Galaxy is the best vehicle for massive, multi-squad attacks. You can probably hold off on this Certification until your character is quite experienced. Early on, you won't have the organizational skills to truly make the most of this behemoth.

Every squad can use one person with this skill, but more than one is overkill.

HARASSER

Certification Point Cost: 2

Prerequisites: —

Prerequisite for: —

Allows Use of: Harasser

The Harasser jeep provides a very nice blend of speed, a bit of firepower, and a bit of multiplayer transport ability (you can bring along one friend). This Certification is cheap—useful for scouts and other non-MAX squad members who want to add some mobility to their game.

LIGHTNING

Certification Point Cost: 4

Prerequisites: —

Prerequisite for: —

Allows Use of: Lightning

The Lightning one-man tank provides very good speed and decent firepower, making it an excellent choice for players who like to work on their own. Scouts and infiltrators with a Lightning Certification can hop into a vehicle and instantly be transformed from a 90-pound weakling to an open-field threat.

Team-oriented types will get more mileage from heavier assault vehicles.

ASSAULT BUGGY

Certification Point Cost: 3

Prerequisites: —

Prerequisite for: —

Allows Use of: Thresher (VS), Marauder (TR), Enforcer (NC)

The Assault Buggy Certification allows access to the Thresher (Vanu Sovereignty), Marauder (Terran Republic), or Enforcer (New Conglomerate). These two- and three-man vehicles effectively blend speed and firepower, and all are more powerful than the Harasser. They're a useful addition to any squad on the move.

MOSQUITO

Certification Point Cost: 3

Prerequisites: —

Prerequisite for: —

Allows Use of: Mosquito

The Mosquito is a great vehicle for scouts and aerial combatants, especially when harassing infantry or taking down Reavers. As a fast air vehicle, it's completely undaunted by terrain obstacles, so it's excellent for getting from one place to another. It's fast.

This is a one-seater, so this Certification is best for scouts and loners.

ASSAULT TANK

Certification Point Cost: 3

Prerequisites: —

Prerequisite for: —

Allows Use of: MagRider (VS), Prowler (TR), Vanguard (NC)

The Assault Tank Certification gives access to the MagRider (Vanu Sovereignty), Prowler (Terran Republic), and Vanguard (New Conglomerate) tanks.

These vehicles are excellent for team-oriented squad members who plan on attacking well-fortified bases or patrolling the outskirts of friendly bases for enemy vehicles. They can be useful during base assaults, though the tank driver typically stays outside while the team proceeds inside the base.

REAVER

Certification Point Cost: 4

Prerequisites: —

Prerequisite for: —

Allows Use of: Reaver

The Reaver gunship is the only aircraft geared toward taking out ground targets. Players who want to rule the skies, harassing infantry or enemy vehicles, or maybe strafing the defenders camped on an enemy base's walls, need this Certification.

SUNDERER

Certification Point Cost: 3

Prerequisites: —

Prerequisite for: —

Allows Use of: Sunderer

The Sunderer transport vehicle, like the Deliverer, is an excellent choice when you want to take your squad on the road. It's massively armored and heavily armed. The Sunderer seats an entire squad, so it's really the only vehicle you need. The tradeoff is that it's slower than the Deliverer, and lacks the amphibious capability.

WRAITH

Certification Point Cost: 2

Prerequisites: —

Prerequisite for: —

Allows Use of: Wraith

The Wraith is essentially a Basilisk without weapons and with stealth capabilities—but those capabilities only work if the player is wearing an Infiltration Suit. Dedicated stealthy players, such as scouts and hackers, will want the Wraith Certification; it allows them to get around very quickly, yet maintain their stealthy ways. Others won't have much use for it.

EQUIPMENT CERTIFICATIONS

Equipment Certifications allow your character to use specialized tools that the average character can't use. This opens up new possibilities and can make your character extremely desirable to a squad.

HACKING

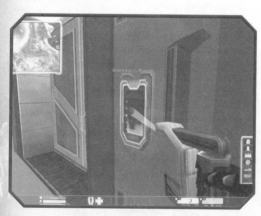

Certification Point Cost: 3

Prerequisites: —

Prerequisite for: Advanced Hacking

Allows Use of: Extra speed and functions for REK

Anyone with a REK (Remote Electronics Kit) who's not in MAX armor can hack. However, those players can only hack doors and Command Consoles. Only players with the Hacking Certification can expand their hacking to other terminals and enemy vehicles. Also, the Hacking Certification speeds up all hacking operations.

This skill is absolutely necessary for any player who plans on hacking anything more than the occasional door, or a Command Console in an emergency.

ADVANCED HACKING

Certification Point Cost: 2

Prerequisites: Hacking

Prerequisite for: —

Allows Use of: Extra speed and functions for REK

Advanced Hacking simply speeds up all hacking operations. It is not critical for the casual hacker, who likes to hack or steal enemy equipment when nobody else is around. It is vital, however, for dedicated hackers who plan to hack Command Consoles in the midst of a firefight or jack enemy AMSes while foes wander around the area. Typical hacking times are reduced by two-thirds with this skill!

Whole character types can be planned around Advanced Hacking. If you love sneaking around and causing trouble, you'll love this Certification.

MEDICAL

Certification Point Cost: 3

Prerequisites: —

Prerequisite for: Advanced Medical

Allows Use of: Medical Applicator

The Medical Certification allows use of the Medical Applicator, a device that heals oneself or others. This is a useful skill on prolonged raids in enemy territory far from an AMS. Healing isn't a particularly flashy job, but medics are welcomed in any squad.

ADVANCED MEDICAL

Certification Point Cost: 2

Prerequisites: Medical

Prerequisite for: —

Allows Use of: Advanced use of Medical Applicator

The Advanced Medical Certification allows you to revive allies from the dead! (You have to get to them before they respawn elsewhere, though.)

This Certification is useful for anyone who already has the Medical Certification—and enjoys it.

ENGINEERING

Certification Point Cost: 3

Prerequisites: —

Prerequisite for: Combat Engineering

Allows Use of: BANK, Nano Dispenser

The Engineering Certification allows you to repair player armor with the BANK (Body Armor Nanite Kit) and to repair equipment and vehicles with the rifle-sized Nano-Dispenser.

Engineering skills are in demand. Aside from the fact that you can repair squadmates' armor (very useful, especially for highly armored characters like MAXes), there's nothing worse than losing your base's Generator and not having anyone to fix it.

Also, Engineering skills help keep an AMS or other vehicle intact in the face of sporadic attacks.

COMBAT ENGINEERING

Certification Point Cost: 2

Prerequisites: Engineering

Prerequisite for: —

Allows Use of: ACE

Combat Engineering allows use of the ACE combat device, a pistol-sized object that deploys into one of four forms: HE Mine, Boomer HE, Motion Alarm Sensor, or Spitfire Deployable Turret.

Like the Hacking Certifications, this Certification opens up a whole new style of play. Choose this if you enjoy placing infrastructure that helps defend your bases.

IMPLANTS

Implants are cybernetic enhancements that temporarily improve your character's performance or provide special skills. There's a maximum of three Implant Slots for any character; these slots are received at Battle Ranks 6, 12, and 18.

You can swap Implants in and out at Implant Terminals, which are found at your Sanctuary and friendly Bio Labs.

Most Implants turn on and off; these Implants drain Stamina while they're active. A few Implants don't drain Stamina, and they are always in effect. Unless otherwise noted in an Implant's description, you can assume that it's the first (Stamina-draining) kind.

ADVANCED REGENERATION

The Advanced Regeneration Implant slowly repairs health, converting two points of Stamina into one health point every moment it's activated. It's too slow to be useful in the middle of a fight, but it's extremely practical for keeping you alive on long missions when there's no medic nearby.

Everyone can benefit from this Implant. It's a convenience more than a necessity, especially if you don't spend much time away from medics or Medical Terminals, but it sure is useful. It's just a matter of whether you'll use something else more.

If your specialization doesn't demand something else, we strongly recommend this Implant.

ADVANCED TARGETING

The Advanced Targeting Implant, while activated, shows you the name and current health of your targeted enemy. It also pops up the names of deployed enemy objects at longer ranges and allows you to see the names of enemies in vehicles.

This may seem like a frivolous Implant, but it's quite helpful for any character who snipes, or characters who spend lots of time fighting infantry. Knowing your enemy's health is useful in a fight. You may think you've done serious damage but you haven't, or vice versa. Knowing an opponent's health level lets you choose the right weapon and tactics to finish the job.

Snipers benefit from this Implant; it lets them select wounded targets to finish off.

The bottom line: This Implant isn't a high priority for most characters, but the extra information benefits snipers and frequent infantry fighters.

AUDIO AMPLIFIER

While active, the Audio Amplifier Implant translates running enemies' footsteps into dots on your Proximity View map. This is an often-underrated Implant.

While sneaking or stationary characters won't show up on Proximity View, running characters will—and players in a fight tend to run a lot. This Implant gives you a real edge in cat-and-mouse battles, providing early warnings of enemies in the area. Often, these early warnings can be parlayed into sneak attacks—and sneak attacks score easy kills.

If your character focuses on infantry combat, you owe it to yourself to experiment with the Audio Amplifier.

DARKLIGHT VISION

The Darklight Vision Implant is arguably the most valuable one for players who spend most of their time on foot. While activated, it reduces your overall field of vision but highlights players in Infiltration Suits, turning them into sitting ducks.

This Implant is crucial if you spend lots of time hunting infantry or guarding bases. Constantly flicking it on and off allows you to keep track of stealthy characters in your base and helps score you lots of easy kills. Better still, it's a way to counter those maddening stealth assassins!

While you can certainly live without this Implant, especially once you've become familiar with stealthy characters' tricks, it's hard to deny its power. Some players always take this as their first Implant and never get rid of it.

MELEE BOOSTER

The Melee Booster is one of the most specialized Implants. While activated, it massively boosts the power of your character's blade weapon—a weapon that is usually too weak to be have an impact. Each swing drains Stamina.

For stealthy characters, this Implant can be very effective. It helps you score stealth kills, freeing up your inventory to carry other devices (such as ACEs, if you're a stealth engineer). Knife kills require no ammo, so you can stay in the field longer. Also, remember that the knife is always accessible (press 5 by default), so you can quickly pull it out even if you're holding a REK in your only pistol slot.

Needless to say, other character types should avoid this specialized Implant.

PERSONAL SHIELD

The Personal Shield Implant is very potent in combat. While it's active it blocks damage, draining one Stamina point for every absorbed damage point.

This device is useful for any fighter, if you remember to turn it on. It's best for heavier armor types that rely more on firepower than on speed, as your Stamina (and hence, your ability to run) can take a beating.

Again, Personal Shield is very powerful in a straightforward fight. Just make sure to get in the habit of using it!

RANGE MAGNIFIER

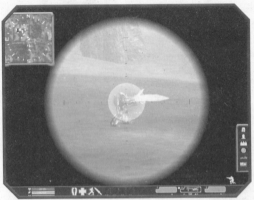

The Range Magnifier is an always-on Implant that doesn't need to be turned on and off. It ups the magnification of any weapon you're using. A weapon that usually sports a 2x magnifier becomes 4x. A 4x weapon becomes 8x. And finally, 8x becomes 12x.

Most weapons aren't accurate enough to really benefit from this enhanced zoom. However, if you're a sniper, or you use reasonably long-range weapons like the Gauss Rifle, the enhanced zoom properties help a lot. Snipers, with their long-range Bolt Drivers, benefit most of all.

For pure scouting purposes, the Range Magnifier shows you enemies at ranges where they're unlikely to see you back.

Snipers and those who fight outdoors often are the likeliest candidates for this Implant. Others won't benefit nearly as much.

SECOND WIND

If you're critically wounded, Second Wind converts Stamina into health points. Often, this keeps you alive just a second or two longer—but that second or two is often decisive.

We really like Second Wind. It's an always-on Implant, so you don't have to worry about flipping it on and off. And anything that prolongs your life in battle (*without* adding more buttons or keys to press) is a good thing.

Every character can benefit from Second Wind. Give it a try; you often won't be aware of it when it's working, but you'll notice that you have a slight edge in most fights.

SILENT RUN

Silent Run is just what it sounds like; it allows you to run without generating any sound. This not only prevents keen-eared players from noticing you, but also prevents players using the Audio Amplifier Implant from seeing you on their Proximity View maps.

Stamina drain for this Implant increases with the bulk of the armor you're wearing.

Stealthy characters with the Silent Run Implant can run when nobody's looking at them without worrying about their footsteps showing up on someone's Proximity View. Other characters usually can do without it.

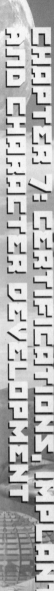

SURGE

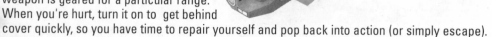

The Surge Implant boosts your character's speed while it's activated. The Stamina drain correlates with the bulk of your armor; lightly armored characters can run for quite a while!

This is another general-purpose Implant that benefits lots of characters. With it, stealthy characters can run past areas they doubt they could sneak past, or elude players who discover them. Fighting characters can close the gap with an opponent or open a bigger gap—both useful techniques, if your weapon is geared for a particular range. When you're hurt, turn it on to get behind cover quickly, so you have time to repair yourself and pop back into action (or simply escape).

Even in non-combat situations, Surge is useful. Impatient base attackers can speed up their run toward the base walls.

Other Implants may be just as useful, or in some cases more useful, but there are *so* many situations in which a speed boost is welcome. We can't help but love this Implant.

CEPS AND COMMAND RANK

Squad leaders receive BEPs for fighting, just like other squad members. When a base is captured, though, the squad leader in charge receives Command Experience Points (CEPs) instead of BEPs.

Accumulate enough CEPs, and you'll increase your Command Rank. The following table shows the CEP thresholds needed to reach each Command Rank and the benefits provided by those ranks.

COMMAND RANKS AND BENEFITS

Command Rank	Required CEPs	Benefits
0	0	None
1	10,000	Place Waypoints
2	25,000	Directed Voice Macros, See Friendly Units
3	75,000	Chalkboard, Small Jamming Radius, Commander Chat Channel
4	150,000	Larger Jamming Radius, See Enemies, Continental Broadcast, Bolt from the Blue
5	300,000	Largest Jamming Radius, Larger See Enemies, Intercontinental Commander Broadcast, Larger Bolt from the Blue

We'll explain the benefits of each Command Rank in the next few sections. Most benefits require the Command Uplink Device, a tool that players without any Command Rank are forbidden to even carry!

NOTE

In addition to the benefits described here, your character's uniform receives an additional, decorative piece of armor with each Command Rank you earn.

COMMAND RANK 1 BENEFITS

At Command Rank 1, characters receive the following benefit.

SQUAD WAYPOINTS

The commander can place up to four waypoints on the main map. These waypoints, useful for giving directions, are visible to everyone in the squad.

NOTE

Placing a fifth waypoint removes the first one.

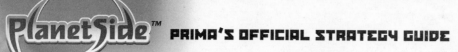

COMMAND RANK 2 BENEFITS

Two new benefits become available to a character attaining Command Rank 2.

DIRECTED VOICE MACROS

Instead of using voice macros that everyone in the squad can hear, you can direct voice commands to individuals or subsets of your squad. This allows you to quickly give custom orders to squad members.

SEE FRIENDLY UNITS

Every 20 minutes, you can use your Command Uplink Device (from the map interface) to get a snapshot of every friendly unit on the continent. Friendly units flash green, then dim to indicate that the information is no longer fresh, fading completely after five minutes.

This extremely valuable command shows the distribution of your forces on the continent, highlighting which areas are weak or unguarded.

COMMAND RANK 3 BENEFITS

At Command Rank 3, an even more powerful set of abilities becomes available.

CHALKBOARD

This ability lets you draw directly on the overhead map. Your sketches can be seen by your squad (if you're using the Squad chat setting) or other commanders (on the Command chat setting).

The Chalkboard lets you quickly and effectively illustrate a battle plan, without repeating complex explanations several times.

JAMMING RADIUS (SMALL)

Every 20 minutes you can emit a pulsed jamming field from your Command Uplink Device. The field lasts 5–10 minutes and creates an umbrella of energy that prevents enemy commanders from seeing you with their See Enemies ability.

The jamming field travels with you; it's big enough to conceal a small vehicle convoy.

NOTE

Enemy commanders *will* see that jamming is taking place. They'll know there's something in that area—but they won't know who or what it is.

COMMANDER CHAT

Command Rank 3 entitles you to use the Commander Chat channel. This channel broadcasts to other Command Rank 3 and higher commanders on the continent. It's very useful for coordinating massive attacks and figuring out what's happening in other parts of the continent.

COMMAND RANK 4 BENEFITS

At Command Rank 4, commanders reach elite status. They have access to a variety of new and enhanced powers.

JAMMING RADIUS (MEDIUM)

The Jamming Radius command from Command Rank 3 is enhanced. Now the jamming field is as big as a facility's default-sized Sphere of Influence.

SEE ENEMIES (SMALL)

This command reveals enemies on the map. The commander uses the map and the Command Uplink Device, and indicates a spot on the continent. All enemies within a certain radius are revealed; they appear as bright red dots, which fade as the information becomes old. They're gone within five minutes.

You can use this power every 20 minutes. Be aware that enemy commanders may jam your efforts with their Jamming Radius ability.

CONTINENTAL BROADCAST

At Command Rank 4, commanders can broadcast messages to *every friendly player* on the continent! This extremely powerful tool helps mobilize big groups and directs extra aid to embattled locations.

BOLT FROM THE BLUE (SMALL)

The commander can now summon an extremely powerful energy bolt from the Orbital Station. The bolt can destroy just about any infantry or vehicles, within a limited radius (around 20 meters) of the target area.

To use this ability, select the appropriate setting on the Command Uplink Device, point at the target area, and press and hold the Fire button for a few moments. You'll receive confirmation, and within 10 seconds the bolt strikes.

Wield this power when dealing with entrenched enemies, large groups of vehicles, or other static targets that are hard to assault otherwise.

COMMAND RANK 5 BENEFITS

At Command Rank 5, you're the best of the best. Your ability to communicate and direct players is unmatched, and you have a wide array of powerful tools at your disposal.

JAMMING RADIUS (LARGE)

The large Jamming Radius is the same as the Rank 3 ability, but it covers an area the size of an Amp Station–enhanced Sphere of Influence.

SEE ENEMIES (LARGE)

This is the same as the Rank 4 ability, except that you can see a larger area (about one-fifth of a continent) with this version.

INTERCONTINENTAL BROADCAST

With this ability you can talk to all commanders of Rank 3–5 in the entire game world—not just on your continent. This is the ultimate rallying tool, allowing you to call in help from other continents.

BOLT FROM THE BLUE (LARGE)

This is just like the Rank 4 ability of the same name, except that the bolt can now cover half of a base's courtyard. It's the ultimate destructive tool, a fitting reward for a commander who's reached the pinnacle of *PlanetSide* status.

CHAPTER 8: COMBAT

As you'll soon realize, much of your battlefield success in *PlanetSide* is based on the situation and your level of preparation, rather than your reflexes. If you use the wrong weapon for the situation, if you don't know the capabilities of your opponent's gear, or if you're outnumbered, combat will seem difficult. On the other hand, if you stick with your squad, know your role, and equip the right gear, you can be effective even if your individual skills are weak.

This chapter deals with both individual and team skills. Much of its advice will seem like simple common sense, because it *is*. But these things must be said, as it's very easy to get impatient and fling your common sense into the nearest ditch. Whenever you find yourself running toward the nearest battle with no real plan of attack, it's your job to pause for a moment, take a deep breath, and consider your tactics. If you can do that, you're well on your way to becoming a superior fighter.

DECIDE WHETHER TO FIGHT

Before launching yourself into a battle zone, it pays to consider your priorities. What are you trying to achieve? Do you stand a chance? Unlike some pure action games, in which kills are the sole measure of success, *Planetside* doesn't reward raw carnage above all else.

UNDERSTAND THE WEAPON AND ARMOR HIERARCHIES

It's crucial to understand what your armor and weapons are capable of, and what the armor and weapons of your opponents are capable of. Lacking that knowledge, it's impossible to make good decisions.

We strongly recommend a thorough read of chapters 2 and 3. When you've absorbed most of the material in those chapters, you'll be ready to decide whether you're at an advantage or a disadvantage in any given fight.

Without that knowledge, you'll be fairly ineffective. Consider: You're running through the forest in an anti-infantry MAX, and three Terran Republic soldiers attack you—one's in a Light Exosuit and firing a Mini-Chaingun, one's in Reinforced Body Armor and firing a Rocklet Rifle, and the last one is a MAX (apparently an anti-aircraft configuration). Which enemy is the biggest threat? Which one is the quickest kill?

Your actual tactics in this theoretical battle will depend on the available cover and on who's closest—but if you have no idea which weapons and armor types are strongest (or you can't identify those weapons and armor types in the first place), you're at a profound disadvantage.

NOTE

By the way: All things being equal in our little scenario, we'd take down the Mini-Chaingun foe first, who is fragile and carries a wicked weapon. Then the Rocklet Gun opponent, then the MAX. It's nearly impossible to win a one-on-three fight if the enemy is competent, but if you proceed in this order, you can realistically take down the two lighter opponents.

ABANDON HOPELESS SITUATIONS

If you're sneaking around in an Infiltration Suit, there's not much you can do to an enemy in MAX armor (unless you happen to know that he or she is seriously injured). Even if you have the advantage of surprise and unload your comparatively puny weapons, you won't do much real damage. When the MAX finally finds you, all it takes is a couple of shots to finish you.

In this situation, the best choice is not to fight at all. Don't reveal yourself—and if you're seen, run. You can take on other enemies effectively, but not this one.

Other situations are equally difficult, but the odds are not as clear-cut. When facing multiple opponents, for example, it can be hard to tell how many there are and what they're all equipped with.

We don't recommend fleeing just because there are unknown factors; if you did that, you'd almost never fight! Also, fleeing is only effective if you have the speed and durability to escape. Fleeing from a faster enemy, or fleeing along an open path that exposes you to excessive shots in the back, is not advisable. But you *should* avoid combat if you clearly aren't prepared for the situation and you have the means to avoid it.

NOTE

Running into combat with a Standard Exosuit and a Suppressor is the ultimate newbie move! We don't recommend it. Go gear up before trying to fight *anyone*.

BE EFFECTIVE WITHOUT FIGHTING

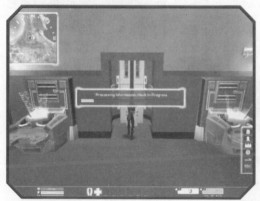

Even if you choose to flee (or not engage the enemy in the first place), you can still be effective. For example, if you discover an enemy AMS but don't have the firepower to take it out, let your squad know it's there. Mark it on the map if you have the appropriate Command Rank to do so, or just tell them it's at your position. They can check the map and see where you are, and then come help you destroy it.

Similarly, if you're hiding in an Infiltration Suit and there's an enemy MAX nearby, tell your squad about it. Let them fight it; meanwhile, seek out lightly armored targets that you *can* effectively fight.

AVOID COMBAT ZONES

If you're on a specific mission that does not involve slugging it out in the field, avoid the battlefield entirely. Sometimes this means taking roundabout paths and going well out of your way.

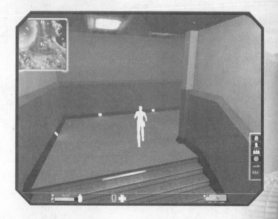

The extra time this requires can be justified, because running through an area where combat is taking place will probably distract you (at the very least) or kill you (at the worst), and your mission is not likely to get completed. Taking the long way is better than getting gunned down four times in a row as you try to take the direct route.

FIRING WEAPONS

The two most basic elements of combat are moving and shooting. We'll cover shooting first.

The following tips will help you maximize your damage output and steer you away from rookie mistakes. Later, the section on movement will provide tips on avoiding return damage.

PICK THE RIGHT WEAPON

As we've already suggested, you must become familiar with the weapon and armor stats in chapters 2 and 3. You don't have to memorize the actual values, but you should develop a sense of what weapons work (or don't work) against various targets.

For example, a lot of weapons aren't worth firing at a MAX. Sure, you *can* fire them, and if you have no other option, you should. But if that's the best you have, in many cases you should avoid the MAX by sneaking or running away.

The bottom line: If you don't have the right weapon for the job, consider backing off and looking for reinforcements.

WHERE TO AIM

Here's an important tip, especially for you would-be snipers: *Planetside* doesn't take body locations into account when calculating hit damage. In other words, a head shot deals the same damage as a torso shot or a leg shot.

The lesson is clear: Aim for the body whenever possible. It's the biggest target, and shots that miss high or low might still hit the head or a leg. Also…well, there just isn't any incentive to aim for anything else.

TIP

When firing weapons that deal splash damage, aim low. Hitting the ground near the target can be almost as damaging as a direct hit.

CONE-OF-FIRE CONSIDERATIONS

Planetside weapons have a "cone-of-fire" effect. Draw an imaginary cone out from the barrel of your weapon; the cone starts out small but gets bigger and bigger at longer range. This cone depicts the possible trajectory of any projectiles fired from the weapon.

The spread of the cone varies from weapon to weapon. Some weapons, such as the precise Bolt Driver, have a very tight cone that ensures good accuracy over extreme range. Others, such as the AMP rapid-fire pistol, have a much wider cone of fire and are therefore less accurate over range.

NOTE

bullets rather than a stream of individual shots, lose more accuracy over distance than other weapon types. Instead of firing single projectiles that may follow any given path within the firing cone, you're firing multiple projectiles at once, all of which *do* take different paths within the cone. As a result, you're more likely to score a partial hit but less likely to deal maximum damage. Use these weapons at close range!

In addition to the "default" cone, your actions have a big effect on the cone size. Crouching while you fire reduces the cone, making weapons more accurate. Running greatly widens the cone, rendering most weapons wildly inaccurate over medium to long range. Firing long bursts makes your weapon progressively more inaccurate, as does getting hit by enemy fire.

The next few sections explain how to use specific techniques to improve your weapon accuracy.

ACCURACY HIERARCHY

How can you improve your accuracy? Here's a hierarchy of movements that affect your cone of fire and, hence, your accuracy. The hierarchy goes from most accurate to least accurate.

1. Crouching, Not Moving
2. Standing, Not Moving
3. Walking
4. Running or Crouch-Walking
5. Jumping

As you can see, the more you move, the less accurate your shots are. Jumping results in such a massive loss of accuracy that you shouldn't bother firing while jumping, except perhaps at a point-blank enemy, with a weapon that doesn't require much accuracy (for example, a shotgun).

SHORT, CONTROLLED BURSTS

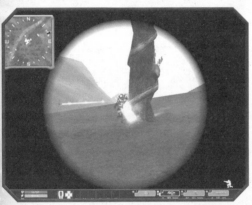

If your weapon permits rapid fire, don't assume that the best technique is to hold down the fire button until the ammo runs dry. Short, controlled bursts are the key to maintaining accuracy.

Get in the habit of firing a burst, moving, and then stopping and firing again. Keep the number of shots fired per burst fairly low. This technique keeps you moving but doesn't sacrifice accuracy.

The exception to this guideline is when the target is very close. In that case, it's much easier to hit—even if you're moving or firing long bursts. Fire nonstop at close-range targets.

DON'T STAND AND TAKE A BEATING

If the enemy has a great line on you and is absolutely destroying you, move before your armor and health run out. However, if you're in heavy armor and your opponent is in light, it can be tempting to stand and take it, because you figure you can drop your enemy first.

That's a valid strategy, but realize that getting hit with a constant, accurate stream of fire widens your own cone of fire. That means you might not be hitting as much as you think you are. It might be time to move behind cover, reload, and reconsider your tactics.

COMBAT MOVEMENT AND TACTICS

Shooting is only half of the equation. What should your feet be doing while you're engaged in a gunfight? After reading the next several sections you should have a few ideas on the subject.

CONSTANT RUNNING: NOT IN VOGUE

Action games that don't incorporate a cone-of-fire system encourage you to run and gun; there's no penalty for running and hopping like a jackrabbit. In fact, wild movement is encouraged; the faster and less predictably you move, the harder you are to hit. And your ability to hit the enemy doesn't suffer a bit!

Constant movement will also make you hard to hit in *Planetside*, but due to the cone of fire effect, your aim will suffer immensely. While running you *will* be more difficult to hit than if you were standing still, but it'll be easier for a standing or crouching enemy to hit you than it will be for you to hit your foe.

The end result? Constant running and jumping will render you ineffective. You're better off using real-world tactics, like running from one piece of cover to the next and firing from cover (not as you run).

CROUCH BUT DON'T CRAWL

The only real surprise in the accuracy hierarchy is that walking while crouching affects your shots just as much as running.

The moral is simple: By all means crouch for extra accuracy, but when it's time to move, get back up and run. Crouch-walking just gives you the worst of both worlds (slow movement plus inaccuracy).

An exception to this rule is when you're behind partial cover (say, a low crate) and crouch-walking allows you to move around without exposing yourself to enemy fire. In that case, it's a very effective method of movement.

NOTE

Crouch-walking is also a good way for a sneaking player in an Infiltration Suit to force him- or herself to move slowly, keeping a very low profile. Since it's a slow method of moving, it also keeps the player invisible to Spitfire Turrets and Motion Detectors.

USE COVER

If you're used to adrenalized, run-and-gun action games, the concept of cover takes some getting used to. In those other games cover is meaningless because everyone can run and jump while maintaining perfect accuracy. Furthermore, everyone tends to move at ludicrous speeds. These two factors make cover inconsequential; why try to hide behind something when your opponent can run and leap to get a better view of you, meanwhile shooting with pinpoint accuracy?

In *Planetside*, however, cover is an effective device. If you patiently stand behind a pile of crates and fire at your opponent, periodically ducking while you reload, you're certain to absorb less damage than if you were out in the open. The cone-of-fire system prevents your enemy from perfectly targeting your head, and the crates will absorb stray shots that would otherwise hit your body.

If your opponent tries to charge around the crates, you can take a number of free shots—and your running attacker's accuracy will be terrible. Usually these factors are enough to win you the battle.

RUN AROUND IN CLOSE COMBAT

There's an exception to the "don't constantly run" rule, which we've already touched on. Battles at extremely close range don't require much accuracy, so you can (and should) run around like crazy when you're fighting up-close and personal. Just remember to tone it down when you're back to fighting at medium and long range.

ZOOM IN WHILE TRAVELING

Everyone can zoom in at least 2x, and players in MAXes (or with high-zoom weapons) can zoom in more. Make a habit of zooming in and out while you cross open ground. This allows you to identify enemies from farther away than you otherwise would. It can give you the early initiative, letting you slide behind cover to initiate a sneak attack or to simply take a detour and avoid whomever you spotted.

WATCH YOUR STAMINA

Keep track of your Stamina while you move around and fight. Stamina might not seem like a big deal until you start to use Implants, or until you find yourself incapable of running in a tense situation. Then you realize that you often take it for granted.

Stamina automatically regenerates whenever you're standing still. Running won't drain Stamina, but it prevents you from regaining it. Jumping burns five Stamina points, and Implants burn Stamina at various rates.

You can't run or activate your Implants if your Stamina is under 20, and you can't jump if it's below five.

Stamina shouldn't rule your battlefield strategy, but you should occasionally make small concessions to it. If your Stamina is low, for example, wait a few extra moments before bursting through a door or making the final approach toward an enemy AMS. You never know when the ability to run away or use an Implant will make the difference between success and failure.

PUTTING IT ALL TOGETHER

Your exact tactics should be flexible, varying based on the situation. Here are a few recommendations for specific scenarios.

FIGHTING HEAVIER OPPONENTS

If you're in an Agile Exosuit and fighting Reinforced Body Armor, or in Reinforced Body Armor and fighting a MAX, you're at a distinct disadvantage. Here are some tips for staying alive.

- Move more than you would against an opponent with equal armor. Use cover more. Fire very quick bursts, then get away. Try to frustrate your opponent into running after you and exposing him- or herself to open shots.

- Look for help. As you fight, look for opportunities to slowly retreat toward friendly soldiers. The more targets your opponent has to deal with, the better.

- Try for the stealth attack as much as possible. Getting in the first shot is particularly necessary when fighting MAXes; their armor is so tough that you need every advantage you can get.

- Maintain distance. Big, slow, heavy-hitting enemies like to get close and destroy you quickly. Fight a retreating battle, using cover as much as possible, and choose a weapon that's accurate in long-range combat.

- If you must fight in close, quickly circle the opponent—especially one in a MAX. Capitalize on the MAX's slow turning speed.

- Don't be afraid to retreat. Any way you slice it, you're at a disadvantage when you're in lighter armor. Don't fight if the situation turns hopeless.

FIGHTING LIGHTER OPPONENTS

When you're in heavy armor and your opponent is in lighter protection, press home your advantage. Here are some tips for dealing with these situations.

- Advance while fighting. You probably have heavier weapons, and you want to use them. The exception is when you're in a MAX and the opponent has powerful armor-piercing missiles. Then, maintain longer range so you can dodge those missiles.

- Don't be completely predictable. If your opponent is skillful at leading you across the map, then shooting you while you're trying to catch up, take a moment and gather yourself. Grab a longer-range weapon if you can and zoom in for a couple of long shots.

- If you're in a MAX, alternate regular running with your Autorun mode (and jumping if you're in a Vanu MAX). You can use this mode to flush an opponent out of cover. Deactivate it before you're actually in firing position, as it takes a few moments to revert to normal (firing) mode.

- Don't spare the ammo. Your advantage lies in having lots of armor and big guns; use both as fully as possible.

- If you're in a MAX, and an opponent circles you so fast that you're having trouble keeping up, run backward to create a little separation. Once you've done that you should get a clean shot.

- Concentrate on accuracy over protection. You have the luxury of extra armor, so you can take a few hits. Don't be afraid to crouch or stand immobile if it lets you get in some accurate shots.

FIGHTING EVENLY MATCHED OPPONENTS

If your opponent is similarly armored, the victor is usually the one who manages weapons and equipment best, and uses the smartest tactics. Here are some suggestions.

- Pay careful attention to range, and pick the right weapon for that range.
- If your opponent is using a specialized weapon that's very range-specific (say, a Jackhammer or a Bolt Driver), pick a more general-purpose weapon and move to a range that's unsuitable for your opponent's weapon.
- If your opponent is using a general-purpose weapon, move in close and use a specialized short-range weapon (such as a Jackhammer or Mini-Chaingun).
- Don't run out of cover if it exposes you to heavy fire. Make your opponent do that. Be patient enough to stand back and fire from your current position.
- Change weapons in mid-fight; your opponent seldom expects this and usually fails to adjust weapons or tactics to match your move. The classic example is to run behind a corner and switch from a general-purpose weapon to a shotgun-style weapon, then let loose when your opponent chases you. You could also run out to longer range (using cover, of course) and switch to a more accurate weapon.
- Don't be afraid to retreat from your position and approach from another angle. Your opponent will often assume that you've simply left the area, and you'll get a chance to score a surprise attack.
- If you run around a corner or behind a big piece of cover, your opponent is sure to have a gun trained on the spot where you're likely to reappear. Don't get impatient and pop back out to see what's going on. Equip a weapon based on your distance from the corner or cover, and dare your opponent to come around it.
- Use indirect-fire weapons like the Thumper or Lasher to break up entrenched battles.

USING HEALTH AND DEFENSIVE ADVANTAGES

The use of gadgets and gear often determines a battle's outcome. For example, if two identical MAXes are slugging it out, toe to toe, they'll usually deal similar damage to each another. The eventual victor may be the one whose aim is slightly better, or the one who got in the first few shots. *Or*, it may be the one who uses jumping (Vanu Sovereignty) to avoid a barrage, or a shield (New Conglomerate) to absorb some damage, or the Spike (Terran Republic) ability to increase accuracy and rate of fire.

Similarly, the use of Medkits, or healing or defensive Implants, often means the difference between success and failure.

Make sure that the keys corresponding to various health-conserving and health-replenishing gadgets are easy to reach; remap them if they aren't. Then, force yourself to use them! It's easy to get caught up in aiming, shooting, and running around, but you must remember to use your special gear as well. You can be certain that your opponent is.

KEEP YOUR FOCUS

It's easy to forget that there are objectives in *Planetside* beyond racking up kills. When you find yourself repeatedly gunned down, respawning in a nearby AMS, and then running out to rejoin the fight in the field nearby, stop and ask yourself if you're getting anything done.

The lure of nearby combat can be strong. Even if you go in with the best of team-oriented intentions, it's easy to get caught in a kill-or-be-killed respawning cycle that resembles a gambling addict pulling a slot-machine lever. You just keep going back for more, even though it's a mindless endeavor.

That's okay for a little while, but you should eventually seek out good squads that maintain a focus on clear goals; stick with those squads as they pursue their goals. You'll get more done this way, advance in Battle Rank faster, and get respect faster. Always remember: Capturing or defending a facility is much more valuable, in game terms, than the outcome of any individual battle.

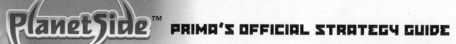

FIGHTING IN AND AGAINST VEHICLES

The battlefield changes considerably with the addition of heavy machinery. When a new enemy vehicle enters the fray, assess it and decide whether it's a priority. Similarly, when driving a vehicle, you must decide whether to fight or drive away from individual situations.

Here are some tips that should help your decision-making process.

WHEN A VEHICLE SHOWS UP, AND YOU'RE ON FOOT...

The first order of business when a vehicle appears (and you're on foot) is to seek cover. Forests and boulders are ideal, but rough terrain (steep hills, cliffs) works also. Standing in the open while fighting a vehicle is suicidal, as all vehicles have reasonable armor, and many have good weapons. Even those with no weapons can run you down, provided that the terrain is right.

If you're not in a MAX and you don't have specific anti-vehicle weapons (such as the Lancer, Striker, or Phoenix), you generally shouldn't fight any vehicle with an actively manned weapon, unless you're very confident of the terrain and your abilities (or you have no choice). If you're forced into a fight, hide behind cover as much as possible; often, you can frustrate the vehicle driver this way.

If you're in a MAX—especially one that's specifically designed to take down the type of vehicle you're facing—you can fight just about anything. However, you'll still need cover, especially when fighting heavily armed and armored vehicles like tanks and Reavers. Remember; despite your heavy armor, a vehicle can still run you down! Use your Autorun mode to get to cover, if necessary. Then fight from a position of strength.

When fighting vehicles, err on the side of caution; pop out of cover infrequently. Take advantage of the fact that the vehicle has a big turning radius, and that the weapons sometimes won't turn quickly in their turrets.

NOTE

Become familiar with the turning limits of various vehicle-mounted weapons; the best way is by testing these weapons yourself. You'll learn their limitations, such as the inability of guns on a Sunderer or Deliverer to aim *down* at nearby targets. Knowing those limitations is extremely useful in a fight!

Always use anti-vehicle (armor-piercing) bullets. If you aren't carrying any, make a point of doing so in the future. Using standard ammo on vehicles can be an exercise in frustration.

If there's a group of friendly units in the area, you can be less cautious, because you probably won't be the sole focus of the vehicle's attention. You can spend more time shooting and less time hiding.

Anyone can shoot at weaponless vehicles or vehicles that are missing gunners. But always be ready to flee if they try to run you down.

WHEN FACING MIXED GROUPS OF VEHICLES AND INFANTRY

If your squad is fighting a mixed group consisting of vehicles and infantry, a good policy is (naturally) to get to cover quickly. Screen yourselves from the vehicles as best you can, while taking down the more fragile, maneu-verable infantry first. Then concentrate on the vehicles.

You can do things in reverse if your squad has good anti-vehicle weapons. Or, you can simply use cover against whatever enemies are easiest to block and fire at whatever remains, be it vehicle or infantry.

If you're constantly facing groups with more combat vehicles than your squad has, consider bringing more combat vehicles along next time or sticking to areas with lots of cover.

DRIVING A COMBAT VEHICLE

If you're in charge of a vehicle that's headed into combat, your strategy should be based on the type of vehicle you've got and your opposition.

If you're in a vehicle with no weapons (such as a Wraith), or if you don't have anyone manning your vehicle's weapons, try to mow down individual soldiers or harass small groups. Anything more involved should be avoided.

If you're in a fragile vehicle, either with or without weapons (say, a Harasser), confine yourself to making a few passes at the enemy. If you can't mow down or gun down all of your enemies in a short period of time, then it's probably time to drive away. There's a limit to how much abuse those vehicles can take.

Tanks, Reavers, and other well-armed, well-armored vehicles can take on small groups of infantry. However, keep a sharp lookout for anti-vehicle MAXes and soldiers with anti-vehicle rocket weapons. These enemies can chew through your armor quickly, especially if you're facing several of them.

The best policy for large fights is to stay within reach of friendly infantry. It's easy to think you're invincible and separate from your infantry, but it's a fact that a mixed force of vehicles and infantry is much harder to deal with than vehicles alone. The friendly infantry will draw fire that would otherwise all go toward you, and the infantry will have an easier time dealing with small, elusive targets that have ensconced themselves in deep cover.

TEAM FIGHTING TECHNIQUES

If you're fighting solo too often, it's time to reconsider your tactics. Anyone who isn't scouting, stealth-hacking, or performing some other sneaky solo endeavor should keep teammates nearby as much as possible.

You'll often win or lose based not on your personal skills but on sheer numbers. If you have more allies than enemies in the vicinity, your chances are good. If you're outnumbered, you're probably on your way out. Sometimes it's just that simple.

STICK TOGETHER-BUT NOT *TOO* TOGETHER

This first rule is obvious, but it bears repeating: Don't get separated from your team, especially during the initial push of a base raid. It's very easy to get separated, since different armor types run at different speeds, and because some players will undoubtedly want to break off to deal with targets of opportunity. Resist these forces as much as humanly possible, because you're stronger if you stick together.

This rule is particularly key for the lighter, faster armor types. If they get too far ahead of the heavier fighters, they're likely to get mowed down. If they come into a battle *after* the heavier fighters, on the other hand, they're less likely to be targeted and immediately annihilated.

While togetherness is desirable, standing too close together, especially when the enemy is using explosive weapons, is a bad idea. Packing several team members behind a small piece of cover, for example, exposes everyone to splash damage. Also, it's easy to get in your teammates' way and become a casualty of friendly fire.

A good rule of thumb is to stick together while moving but spread out a bit when actual combat begins. If everyone has his or her own bit of cover, it not only reduces the risk of extensive splash damage and friendly fire, but it makes your squad harder to flank. Also, it's harder for the enemy to keep their eyes on everyone at once, and that's a good thing.

MAINTAIN MIXED GROUPS

Groups consisting of all light or all heavy armor are usually inferior to mixed groups. Mixed groups have a good assortment of skills and are able to do things like hack vehicles, heal teammates, and repair armor. They can also carry a wide assortment of weapons, which gives them combat versatility.

That said, if you *must* load up on one armor type, you'll have an easier time at the actual fighting part of your mission if you load up on MAXes and other heavy armors. Having no MAXes (or only one MAX) is a recipe for failure, as defenders that do have MAXes will tear your squad to ribbons.

The downside of too many MAXes comes when your team needs to perform non-combat activities (healing, repairing, driving) and cannot.

HAVE ANTI-VEHICLE AND ANTI-PERSONNEL WEAPONS

Squad members in Reinforced Body Armor provide the squad with its versatility. They should have both anti-vehicle and anti-personnel weapons ready at all times. When a fight starts, they should break out the appropriate weapons and lend a hand to the MAXes.

The very lightest squad members, especially those in Infiltration Suits, should try to flank the enemy and score cheap surprise kills. Or, they can take advantage of the distraction and hack or destroy a nearby objective.

BE AWARE OF WHO'S TARGETED

Keep track of which squad member is drawing the most fire. Ideally, the MAXes should be up front, drawing most of the enemy's fire. Meanwhile, the more maneuverable squad members should take advantage of the enemy's preoccupation with the MAXes. They should flank the enemy if possible and take advantage of opponents' distraction to get in a few clean shots.

If you're not currently a target, concentrate on accuracy. Crouch or stand still; there's no need to hurry if you're not being shot at. Deliver the most damage you can, as accurately as you can, and move only when your opponents' focus shifts to you.

STEP BACK WHEN INJURED

If you take a beating and get seriously hurt, retreat behind cover and let your squad pick up the slack. Wait until the enemy's focus is on someone else before popping back out to take another shot. Heal yourself while you're back there if you have any items or Implants that will help you.

If enemies smell blood, they may try to charge your position. Be prepared for this, aiming at the most likely spot of the charge. Be sure that your best close-range weapon is equipped.

FLANK IF POSSIBLE

Lighter armor types need to stay in motion. If they stand motionless and cluster up with the MAXes, the group is easy to keep track of. Active flanking allows the lighter squad members to reach better cover and get better shots. It also forces the opponent to constantly scan the area and keep track of the various members of your squad—and the more they need to keep track of, the more difficult it is for them to fight effectively.

LEARN YOUR SQUAD

Your combat proficiency will increase if you play with the same group all the time. You'll learn everyone's favorite weapons and techniques, and that knowledge translates to increased confidence when you fight.

Even if you don't know your squad that well, at least knowing that they're competent players is a real asset. When you're playing with competent players, you know they won't run off and abandon you. You know if you duck behind cover, hurt, they're likely to pick up the slack. These things are important when playing in a confusing and crowded environment.

KEEP YOUR EYES OPEN

Awareness is not just a key to battlefield success—it's also a key to improving.

If you get killed but don't know who or what got you, study the message area. Knowing the weapon and player that dropped you is very useful. For example, you may have been sniped from afar; this will become clear if the weapon in question was a Bolt Driver. Or, a sneaky character in an Infiltration Suit might have shot you in the back. This is likely if the killing weapon was an AMP or Scatter Pistol.

Awareness extends to studying your most skillful teammates. What gear do they use? What tactics do they use when they fight? Emulating better players is a surefire path to success.

Don't forget to study your opponents, either. What sort of enemies consistently beat you, and what sort of gear are they using? Are they winning because they're using gear specifically designed to defeat *your* gear? Or are they using a particular tactic or technique that you can't deal with?

Studying other players is also useful for learning new tricks. If you only use the Vanu MAX's jumping ability to get up and down from high places, you might be surprised when you find someone who uses that skill effectively in combat.

Watch that player carefully, and determine whether you could use those moves the next time you fight.

Imitation is not only the sincerest form of flattery; it's also the fastest path to improvement.

PRIMA'S OFFICIAL STRATEGY GUIDE

CHAPTER 9: TEAM STRATEGY

Your main goals in *PlanetSide* are to form an effective combat group and expand your Empire's borders. Claiming new territory and protecting your current holdings are the twin axioms of Auraxis™.

In game terms, this means you'll spend most of your time either attacking or defending facilities. When you're not actively attacking or defending, you should be *preparing* to attack or defend something.

It all sounds very simple, but to succeed you'll need skill, experience, and good technique. This chapter instructs you in techniques for locating and assembling a team, getting to and from a combat site, assaulting bases, defending bases, and other key aspects of the *PlanetSide* experience.

When you're done reading this chapter you won't be a veteran, but you will have a good idea of what to do in most combat situations.

GETTING ORGANIZED

The first order of business is to connect with some allies. We understand if you're skeptical; getting people to cooperate can be tough! Many games have tried and failed in the teamwork department. You may have been told that teamwork was the key in those games, too, but experience taught you otherwise.

PlanetSide has some of the best organizational tools of any game to date; furthermore, there are such overwhelming advantages to getting organized (and corresponding disincentives for going solo) that you will likely find yourself cooperating with others. And, just as important, other players have an equally big incentive to cooperate with you. That means finding willing teammates won't be an exercise in frustration.

YOU NEED HELP!

PlanetSide encourages (some would say demands) teamwork in the following ways:

- There are so many players in the game that a lone attacker or defender will be overwhelmed. Even if an enemy base starts out empty, attacking it triggers a response—and the response will likely include at least one full enemy squad.

- Every character has limitations, due to both armor restrictions and the fact that nobody can be certified in every area. Having teammates around allows you to command a more complete skill set.

- Joining a squad lets you see where specific allies are (on the minimap and the large-scale map) and hear what they're doing (thanks to Squad chat mode). This gives you a much better sense of what's going on in the immediate area and allows you to be more effective.

- Important tasks can't be performed quickly without a team; for example, you can't drive two AMSes up to an enemy installation, blow up an enemy AMS, clear away mines and turrets, and hack into the computer. (Well…you could try, but it'd take forever.)

- You gain experience (BEPs) whenever your squad members gain experience. (You don't share the points; everybody gets their own points.) Because of this mechanism, it's much easier to gain BEPs and Battle Ranks when you're a member of a squad.

It's the combination of teamwork-rewarding gameplay and useful player interaction tools that makes good teamwork so easily attainable.

SQUADS AND OUTFITS

Two social groups are recognized and implemented in the game: squads and outfits.

Squads are comparatively small, temporary groups that band together for the purpose of combining their members' firepower and skills. The result is a (potentially) cohesive group that can act together and be much more effective than the individual members on their own.

Outfits are larger groups; you can think of them as clans or guilds. Whereas squads are temporary, outfits are permanent; the game remembers that you've joined an outfit, even when you log off. Outfits are useful because they're a permanent subgroup of your Empire, which contains people you generally know and trust.

SQUADS IN DETAIL

Squads are temporary groups of up to 10 members. They're formed when a leader uses the /invite command to recruit teammates. They end when the last group member finally logs off (or is kicked out).

When you become a member of a squad, the following things happen:

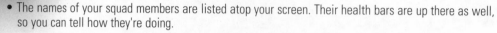

- The names of your squad members are listed atop your screen. Their health bars are up there as well, so you can tell how they're doing.

- When you look at a friendly character, a name appears above that character's head. The name is green, unless it's a squad member; squad members' names are gold.

- Squad members show up on both the Proximity View (a.k.a. radar) and the full-screen map as yellow numbers. (The numbers correlate to numbers assigned to each squad member's name atop your screen.)

- As already noted, whenever a nearby squad member gains experience, you gain the same amount of experience.

- Select the Squad mode on the chat window to send messages to your entire squad. This is the most efficient way of communicating with multiple allies during battle.

MANAGING A SQUAD

Create a squad by inviting other players to join you (type /invite *playername*) in the chat window. Or, set your character to Looking for Squad, and someone may invite you.

To jumpstart the process of getting picked, use the /broadcast chat command to ask everyone in your current SOI if they'd like to join you. Outfit channels can be used for this too. Or, if you see a likely squad leader, /tell *username* to communicate directly with that leader and request an invite.

If you're in charge of your own squad, you can /kick *playername* to get rid of squad members that aren't sticking with the program. Or, to relinquish control (e.g., when you're done for the night), /promote *username* to appoint a different group member leader.

OUTFITS IN DETAIL

An outfit is larger than a squad. It's formed when the leader of a 10-member squad presses the Create Outfit button on the Outfit Information window.

Outfits have their own hierarchy. If you're in charge of one, you can use the Outfit Information window to promote members to various levels, invite new members, kick out old ones, or change the decal that appears on outfit members' uniforms.

170

Aside from the fun social aspect of belonging to a smaller, more tight-knit group within your larger Empire, outfits' main benefit is that they make squad creation and coordination easier.

Join a squad every time you play *PlanetSide*. If you don't belong to an outfit, you probably won't really know too many players; it can be hard to know what sort of players you're getting.

If you join a fairly selective outfit, you can be reasonably assured that the other members of the outfit are competent. At the very least, they've been screened by the outfit's leader, and they met with his or her approval.

Because of these factors, belonging to an outfit allows you to form a squad quickly and effectively. Look for members of your outfit when you create or join a squad; you can be reasonably certain that you're getting good, quality players who know their roles and won't give you a hard time.

NOTE

Outfits are also very useful when you want to form multi-squad attack groups. Multiple squads from the same outfit know they can trust and count on each other, and they are much more likely to coordinate well.

JOIN OR CREATE?

Should you join a squad or outfit, or create one yourself? That partially depends on what sort of player you are and what you like to do. If you really want to lead, feel free to form a squad of your own, and then bind it into an outfit if you like everyone and they're all willing to join.

That said, we recommend being a follower awhile. Most people do best if they learn the game, make some friends, and then join an existing outfit. There's plenty of opportunity to captain your own squad within the structure of the outfit.

PlanetSide™ PRIMA'S OFFICIAL STRATEGY GUIDE

If you do this for a while, and you like command enough that you'd really like to head your own outfit, break away to form a new one (you'll probably take some of your closest friends along with you).

TIP

This sort of thing happens every day in the business world. Most entrepreneurs don't form their own businesses directly out of school; instead, they join an existing company, learn the ropes, make some friends, and then split off with their friends to create a new business.

FINDING THE GROUP FOR YOU

You need to play alongside people to know whether you like them and their approach to the game. Never hesitate to join a squad, even if you don't know anyone. You need to start somewhere.

Be more picky about joining an outfit. Make sure you've dealt with several players from that outfit before joining. Ask yourself these questions:

- Do I *like* these people? You'll have no fun if you're playing with unpleasant people, even if they're effective fighters.
- Am I comfortable with the skill level? If everyone's reflexes are bionic but you're a little slow, you won't have any fun. Ditto if you're great and everyone else lacks skill.
- Am I happy with the level of organization? Some groups play fast and loose, while others are led by drill sergeants. Don't join an outfit if you think it's populated by slackers or control freaks.
- Is there an implicit time commitment? One outfit might expect you to be there every weekday, from 7:00 to 9:00. Another outfit might not care when, or how often, you log in. Make sure you aren't expected to log more time more than you're comfortable with.

BASE ASSAULT 101

Base assaults don't have to be pretty to be effective. In fact, they don't even have to be organized. If you throw enough good players at a base defended by a smaller (or less skillful) group, the base will typically fall.

However, since you grabbed this book, you're probably interested in learning how to do things efficiently and effectively. You want to know how to take a base even if you don't possess overwhelming numbers. In short, you want to learn how to do things the smart way.

The next few sections present effective methods for attacking and capturing a base. They are certainly not the only methods, but they are proven and reliable.

OUTLINE OF AN EFFECTIVE BASE ASSAULT

We must again stress that not every base assault is particularly well planned. If players are experienced enough to know their roles, much of this stuff is just understood, not explicitly communicated. However, this material works as a starting point for planning your own base assaults.

A good base assault includes most of the following steps:

1. Choosing a target
2. Reconnaissance
3. Planning and gathering
4. Vehicle and personnel deployment
5. Neutralizing exterior forces (optional)
6. Base entry (can be stealthy or full-scale)
7. Neutralizing interior forces (may include attacking the infrastructure first)
8. Hacking the Command Console
9. Defending during the capture period
10. Re-equipping, deploying infrastructure, and leaving guards

CHOOSING A TARGET

Any enemy facility is a likely target, but some are better targets than others. Decide what sort of assault you want to perform, and then choose a target that is vulnerable to that assault type.

"Border" facilities that are close to your friendly facilities are a natural choice. However, these facilities are obvious targets and are likely to be well defended. The benefit of attacking these facilities is that even if your attack group's AMSes are all destroyed, and you control no nearby towers, your squad will still respawn within reasonable striking distance. The downside is that these bases tend to be crawling with enemies. A sneak attack can be tough, and a full assault typically requires a lot of manpower.

RECONNAISSANCE

Most attacks take place without any formal recon. However, knowing exactly what you're up against can be remarkably helpful. Are there enemies in the courtyard, or are they all in the basement? Is there anyone patrolling the walls or manning the Wall Turrets? Are the grounds heavily mined and packed with Spitfire Turrets? Is there a full squad in there, or two squads, or just a lone thumb-twiddling MAX?

There a number of ways to benefit from recon. Some require more effort than others, and some are more thorough than others.

An easy way to get basic information is to hang back, preferably near cover, and zoom in on the base from afar. This works best if you have a view of the main base entrance and one of your squad members has a Bolt Driver (which features an excellent zoom lens). Watch the base for a minute. You'll see how much general activity there is, and you'll notice anyone patrolling the walls.

Another form of recon is completely passive: Watch the chat window and monitor your allies' chatter. Often you'll learn that a particular base is empty, or poorly guarded, or swarming with enemies. This can be enough information to act on (or not act on).

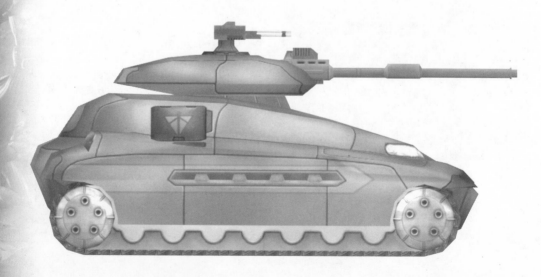

The best form of recon comes when you send a lone scout in an Infiltration Suit into a potential target base. The scout can get exceptionally detailed information on the base interior and exterior.

If the scout is killed, chances are good that there's strong, active resistance; bring a larger attack team than originally intended, or pick a different target. If the scout survives, he or she can lurk inside the base and create a distraction while the main force arrives or start destroying equipment, killing lightly armored enemies, or even hacking the Console (if it's not very well guarded).

PLANNING AND GATHERING

The next task is to get everyone on the same page and in the same place. This sounds easy, but the logistics can be daunting. Anyone who's tried to play an online game cooperatively will know what we mean.

EFFECTIVE PLANNING AND GATHERING

Three things are required to consistently plan good attacks and assemble effective attack teams: a good leader, patience, and experienced, team-oriented squad members.

A good leader is experienced and good at communicating; knows what needs to be brought along for an assault; won't lead an attack on a heavily defended base without enough soldiers for the assault; won't forget to bring an AMS or heavy attack vehicles if the base exterior is well-defended; issues short, clear instructions and waits a reasonable amount of time for everyone to follow them before proceeding to the next task.

Patience is required because, despite everyone's best intentions, you'll have to wait for everyone to assemble. Someone will inevitably get stuck waiting for the HART Shuttle; someone driving a slow vehicle may get stuck or take a wrong turn. If you jump the gun and attack while several of your squad members are straggling across the map, you've put yourself at a big disadvantage.

Finally, you need experienced, team-oriented squad members. By "experienced" we just mean players who have played enough to know the basic game processes, like how to get from one place to another effectively. Your raid will fall apart if people can't figure out how to get to an Equipment Terminal or how to make a particular vehicle work.

By "team-oriented," we mean players who will take orders and stick to the task. If your team contains folks who get sidetracked easily, even the best leader can't keep it together. Some players have no qualms about deserting the main attack group so they can hop into a Wall Turret and fire at a hovering Mosquito, even if that aircraft has no real bearing on the squad's ability to take the base.

PLANNING AND GATHERING LOCALES

The best gathering point is usually a friendly base near the target base. Ideally, this base should be able to create the vehicles you need for the attack. If it can't, you must find another base.

If you lack a nearby base, collect all necessary vehicles at your Sanctuary or on a different planet, and then proceed en masse through a Warp Gate.

A Warp Gate is an excellent starting point for large-scale attacks featuring multiple squads, because you can create the massive Galaxy attack vehicle and ride it to the destination.

VEHICLE AND PERSONNEL DEPLOYMENT

When all participating squads are ready, roll toward the base. Stick together. Straggling into the base in waves is much less effective than arriving in a single mass. For an element of surprise, have everyone hang back while the AMS is deployed and any other preliminaries are taken care of. Then give the green light and advance.

In most cases, you'll want to take control of a nearby tower on your way to the target base. This is typically very easy to do, and it gives you a local respawn point in addition to your AMS. However, this can be a double-edged sword in a stealth attack, as alert enemies will read the notice that you took the tower, and will logically assume that you're staging an attack in the vicinity.

NEUTRALIZING EXTERIOR FORCES

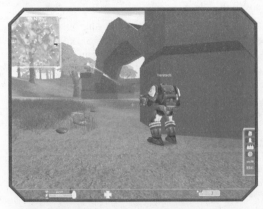

Depending on the amount of enemy resistance and the type of attack you've planned, you may want to beat down the defenders on the base exterior (in the courtyard, on the walls and walkways, and on the rooftops) before making your way inside.

If you've planned a straightforward attack that emphasizes combat over stealth, you'll need to deal with exterior defenses. If you're trying for a straight run at the Command Console, on the other hand, avoid the exterior defenses as much as possible. Ideally, you'll enter through the base's back door.

Assuming that you *do* need to deal with exterior defenses, adjust your tactics based on the size of your attack. In a small- or medium-sized attack against a lightly defended base, rush the courtyard (with combat vehicles first, if you've brought them), pin down or destroy any visible soldiers and Spitfire Turrets, hack the front door, and get inside. Don't follow stragglers or get caught in an endless firefight outside.

In a massive attack, where you plan to dominate the base with lots of troops, vehicles, and firepower, be more methodical. Take down Wall Turrets with anti-vehicle weapons. Drive vehicles into the courtyard, and leave gunners inside so they can take advantage of the vehicles' powerful guns. Hack exterior Vehicle Terminals. Take down all visible Spitfire Turrets.

NOTE

Regardless of your attack style, it's crucial to scout for enemy AMSes and destroy or jack them. The success of your attack hinges on taking down all of the enemy's nearby respawn points (including AMSes and the base itself) while your own AMSes are kept intact. This allows you to eventually turn the tide in your favor.

Regardless of your method, remember that your goal, the Command Console, is inside. Unless you have lots of troops and lots of AMSes in the area, you can't afford to lose many allies outside. Destroy anyone and anything that's a direct threat, and then get inside.

BASE ENTRY

Your method of getting inside the actual base structure depends, once again, on what you're shooting for.

Every base has a back door, and commando-style raids usually work best if you enter this way. Just beware of mines, turrets, and alert defenders.

The ground-level front door is a good option if you're attacking in force and if the Command Console is in the basement. Enter this door and start down the stairs.

If the Command Console is upstairs, many of the defenders will be patrolling the rooftops and upper walkways. You can either get onto the walkways and fight your way inside, or enter through a ground-level door and run up the stairs. The ground-level door is usually a little bit sneakier.

Regardless of the entry point, it helps to know exactly where the Command Console is located, so you can get there quickly. Refer to chapter 6 for standard base blueprints.

NEUTRALIZING INTERIOR FORCES

The first thing to figure out, once inside the base, is where you're going. If you think you have enough firepower to get all the way to the Command Console, hack it, and hold it, go directly there.

If the base has lots of skillful defenders, or if the defenders are really packed around the Command Console, destroy the Generator and/or Respawn Tubes first.

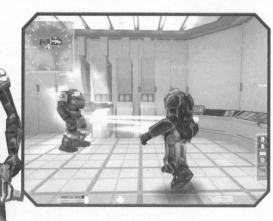

Whether you take out the Generator, Respawn Tubes, or Command Console first, it's important to do it quickly and not get sidetracked by meaningless combat. If a fight starts to get messy, don't be afraid to leave it. Run toward your goal, so that part of your squad can attack or hack the target while the others defend.

Remember that killing enemies is much less meaningful if they can respawn right back into the base. After the Generators or Respawn Tubes are destroyed, or after the Command Console is hacked, taking out enemies is a lot more significant.

HACKING THE COMMAND CONSOLE

You must either completely clear out the enemies around the Command Console and then hack it, or have a hacker in an Infiltration Suit work on it while the rest of the team is busy fighting (and distracting) the enemy.

The faster you hack the Console, the better. A hacked base is neutral for 15 minutes, and a neutral base prevents enemy respawning.

If you're depending on hacking the Command Console to shut down enemy respawning (i.e., you didn't bother to attack the Generator or Respawn Tubes first), then you really need to hack that Console quickly. It helps to have someone with an Advanced Hacking Certification along.

DEFENDING DURING THE CAPTURE PERIOD

Once the Console is hacked, your team needs to hunker down and defend it. Hopefully you brought along some MAXes, as the enemy will probably make a couple of rushes to retake the Console.

Hackers should now hack nearby Equipment Terminals and Medical Terminals, allowing your squad to heal and grab new gear. Light squad members may switch to heavier armor, as defense is now the first priority. Squad members in good combat armor should take defensive positions around the Command Console.

Be sure to heal and repair squad members during lulls in the action.

Lightly armored characters, who specialize in tasks such as hacking and scouting, won't add much to the defenses if they hang around near the Console after it's hacked. Instead, they can spread out in the base to look for enemies. They also can go out to the base walls or rooftops and report incoming foes to the rest of the squad. This intelligence can be very useful for the heavier-armored defenders waiting by the Command Console.

Finally, players in Infiltration Suits can lurk invisibly by the Command Console and take down hackers trying to sneak in (possibly wearing Infiltration Suits too) and re-hack the Console out from under the invasion force.

NOTE

Darklight Vision reveals players in Infiltration Suits. It's a particularly useful skill when you're defending the Command Console from re-hacking.

RE-EQUIPPING, DEPLOYING INFRASTRUCTURE, AND LEAVING GUARDS

After defending the hacked Command Console for 15 minutes, the base is yours. Don't relax, though; the enemy may be mounting a massive force to retake the base!

When the base is turned over to you, heal and re-equip your forces with the base facilities.

Have players with the Combat Engineering Certification deploy HE Mines, Spitfire Turrets, and Motion Sensors all over the base. If you don't have a friendly AMS close by, drive one up or buy one from the Vehicle Terminal and park it in the courtyard. This helps in the event of a sudden counterattack, which can take out your respawning facilities.

Ideally, leave guards at every facility. This is a sticky issue, because while it's strategically useful to guard facilities at all times, nobody wants to sit around on patrol duty, waiting for an attack that might never come.

A good compromise is to wait around for a few minutes after re-equipping and deploying the infrastructure. Once you're relatively certain that the enemy isn't mounting an immediate counterattack, take off and look for another fight. Continually refer to the map; you might need to return later in the event of a counterattack.

BASE DEFENSE 101

Successful base defense doesn't require as much organization as a successful base assault. Just having enough decent players in the base is often enough to thwart a small-scale or poorly planned attack. However, you'll have to step it up when you're outnumbered or facing veteran opponents. These tips will help improve your base defense skills.

SQUADS ARE STILL IMPORTANT

There's a natural tendency to carefully organize for a base assault (which obviously requires some coordination) but to then play it fast and loose on defense.

This is a bad idea. Organize squads for defense, and try to keep them intact. This gives you the same communication and organizational benefits as the attackers.

DEPLOY INFRASTRUCTURE

Spitfire Turret

Spitfire Turrets alone won't kill anyone but the greenest players. Ditto for HE Mines. And Motion Sensors won't do a thing if there's nobody to benefit from them!

Always fill your bases with these items, though, because they do two things. They slow attackers down, which gives you extra time to deal with them, and they force attackers to reveal their position.

A base with no deployed infrastructure is easy for attackers to invade. They can run around without any worries and concentrate on human defenders.

A base packed with infrastructure is very tough to assault. Even if there aren't many defenders, the attackers have to take it a little slower than usual, watching for mines and destroying Spitfire Turrets wherever they appear. The sound and motion caused by attackers destroying infrastructure makes the attackers' position obvious. Defenders are more likely to spot the attackers and get in the first shot while the attackers are busy with the infrastructure.

WATCH THE BIG MAP; WATCH THE PROXIMITY MAP

When you're playing defense, periodically check both the big map and Proximity View.

Watch the big map when you're not busy defending a particular spot. Look for telltale icons next to friendly facilities; the "power out" lightning bolt indicates that the facility is being attacked or contested. And, obviously, the "base hacked" icon is a sure sign that the facility is in trouble. Assemble your squad and go investigate.

When you're defending a particular spot, pay careful attention to Proximity View. Zoom out to the 200-meter range and watch for red dots and icons that indicate enemy soldiers and vehicles. Constant use of Proximity View is a key to battlefield awareness.

FOCUS ON THE EXTERIOR

It's useful to have a few defenders in the vicinity of the Command Console; a small group down there can usually foil a half-baked assault.

It's generally better to have most defenders start on the exterior of the base, though. Specifically, if you have defenders on the walls and walkways, it's much easier to see an invasion force before it arrives and halt it before it makes its way inside. The farther out you can start to provide resistance, the harder it will be for the attackers to succeed.

If you get nervous about the Command Console or the Generator, send someone inside after the fighting begins to call for help if the fighting moves indoors.

NOTE

If most of your defenders are deployed outside, keep a sharp lookout on your base's back door. Be sure that it's mined, deploy Spitfire Turrets near it, and check it frequently. If anyone gets inside, collapse your defenses and deal with the threat.

NOTE

Remember, you have 15 minutes to recapture the base if a hacker does gain control of it. This frees you to fight outside, without worrying so much about a hacker breaching your defenses.

USE WALL TURRETS

Wall Turrets are an excellent reason to stage the first phase of your base defense outdoors. Hop into one for the following reasons:

- They're extremely powerful against both personnel and vehicles.
- They rotate 360 degrees, targeting a much wider range of foes than you might expect.
- They protect the gunner. When someone shoots at the Wall Turret, no damage gets through to the gunner, though the gunner can be killed if the Wall Turret is destroyed.

USE VEHICLES-ESPECIALLY AMSES

Skillful attackers tend to attack in force, and they often bring vehicles. More than just transportation for the raid, these vehicles can lay down covering fire and help the attackers establish control of the courtyard.

As a defender, you have access to vehicles too. Make use of them! The most important thing is to buy an AMS or two and hide them somewhere near the base. That way, if the base is hacked or the Generator or Respawn Tubes are destroyed, defenders can reappear nearby and get right back into the action.

NOTE

Having a deployed AMS on defense often makes the difference between success and failure.

You can also deploy other vehicles for defense. Fly above the base in a Mosquito or Reaver; scout for attackers, and let your team know about them. (And then, attack!)

Drive around the base in a Lightning tank; you might discover an attack force well before it strikes. Again, let your friends know, and then press the attack.

Vehicle purchases can be made in the midst of battle. If the enemy is trying to establish control of the courtyard, go buy a good combat vehicle and hop into the fray; you'll be a lot more effective in a vehicle than on foot.

CALL FOR HELP

Don't be afraid to call for help on defense, especially if you're outnumbered. If you're by yourself, call back the rest of your squad. If your squad is already there, use the /tell command, Outfit chat mode, or Command chat mode (if you're qualified to use it) to ask other squads for immediate help. Ask them to bring an AMS if your base is contested and you don't have an AMS handy.

You'll be amazed at how much better you'll do if you call in reinforcements at the appropriate times.

HUNT ENEMY AMSES

The AMS is the backbone of most base assaults. Without one, fallen attackers will respawn farther away, and attacks are more easily stalled.

If you're faced with an ongoing assault, just gunning down individual soldiers is not going to make it end. Destroying or jacking all of the enemies' AMSes (remember, there may be more than one) is the key to slowing the stream of attackers down to a trickle.

To hunt AMSes, circle the base in ever-widening loops. Watch carefully for enemies running toward your base. They've often just respawned at their AMS, and they're trying to get back into the action.

Run (or drive) to the general area where you think the soldier came from. The AMS is likely to be in the general area; remember that it will only appear if you're right in front of it.

Not everyone should hunt AMSes; only a couple of defenders should do this, while the others defend the base. Scouts in Infiltration Suits are best at finding AMSes, as they can move quickly and avoid combat. MAXes work too, because they can move very quickly (using Autorun mode) and absorb a lot of damage while they search.

Once an AMS is discovered, let your squad know about it. Try to hack it if you're in an Infiltration Suit, or just destroy it. Destroying an AMS works best if you gather a few friends for the attack, or attack using a vehicle with a heavy gun.

FALL BACK TO THE INTERIOR

When your Generator, Respawn Tubes, or Command Console comes under direct assault, it's time to pack in the defense and fight inside. Ideally, a few allies should still scout the area around the base, looking for enemy AMSes. The rest need to hold down the fort until reinforcements arrive.

STEALTH WORKS FOR RE-HACKS!

A lone hacker in an Infiltration Suit is not very effective at capturing enemy bases, even if they're mostly deserted. Sure, the spy can get inside the base and hack the Command Console. But effectively fighting the enemies that are almost certain to respond and re-hack the Console is nearly impossible.

On the other hand, a lone hacker in an Infiltration Suit *can* effectively retake a base during the 15-minute takeover period. That's because control *immediately* reverts to the original Empire if the Control Console is re-hacked during that time.

The difference, obviously, is that the hacker doesn't need to survive after hacking the Console to make the effort worthwhile. A single hacker can recapture the base all alone; this buys some time for reinforcements to arrive.

CHAPTER 10: FINDING A ROLE

PlanetSide is a big game. The world itself is big, the number of players large, and the choices you're presented with—in areas as diverse as weapon and armor selection, picking a squad, and choosing an area to fight—are legion. One important way of dealing with all the chaos is to find a role for your character.

A role is simply a job or set of jobs. Most roles require particular skills, so the role you play goes hand-in-hand with the Certifications you select. This chapter discusses a number of useful roles, along with the Certifications and gear that they require. By the time you're done here, you'll have a better idea of what choices are available and how you want to develop your character.

A FEW WORDS ABOUT ROLES

You may get the impression that roles are mutually exclusive, but they're not. A medic can also be a good fighter; a hacker can also be an infiltrator; and an engineer can also be a driver. There are lots of combinations, some more natural than others. We'll discuss the most natural combinations of roles (such as scout and hacker) at the chapter's end. We'll also suggest some not-so-obvious combinations that work well.

Since one character can play multiple roles, you shouldn't take our guidelines too literally. If we say your squad should include two AMS drivers, for example, we don't mean you should have two characters that literally do nothing but truck across the map with an AMS. We just mean you should have two characters whose skill repertoire includes AMS Certifications. Those characters will obviously play other roles as well.

> **NOTE**
>
> Your roles are quite limited when you first start out; as your character reaches higher and higher levels, though, you'll obtain enough Certification Points to effectively play more than one role. Thanks to your ability to unlearn a Certification, your role can freely adapt over time.

MAXES

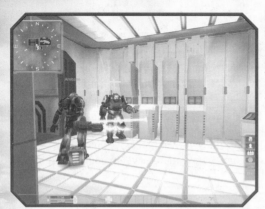

MAXes are not just an armor type; in effect, they are their own role. MAXes have excellent armor and firepower, but they don't allow the use of *any* alternate tools or weapons, and they can't drive vehicles. As a result, a MAX is essentially its own class—a powerful and effective fighting class, but also one that's incapable of diversifying.

TASKS FOR THE ANTI-INFANTRY MAX

Anti-infantry MAXes include the Terran Republic's Dual Cycler MAX, the Vanu Sovereignty's Comet MAX, and the New Conglomerate's Scattercannon MAX.

Anti-infantry MAXes are good fighters, so they can be effective just about anywhere. The following tasks are performed particularly well, however.

INTERIOR BASE ATTACKER

MAXes are not subtle, and they're not terribly versatile. They are, however, indispensable when you're trying to take over a hostile base. You'll need to clear out lots of infantry, and if you don't bring along the big guns and big armor, you'll be mowed down well before you accomplish your goal.

Base defenders have advantages over attackers, and one of their main assets is their ability to generate MAXes on-site, as long as the Generator and Equipment Terminals are in good working order. Attackers can't generate MAX armor in an AMS, so they must be more creative if they want MAXes on their side.

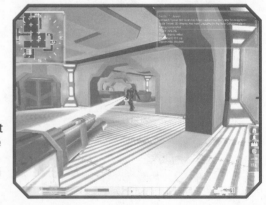

Every squad can benefit from a couple of anti-infantry MAXes. They're useful at any point where you encounter enemy troops, but they're particularly useful when you take the fight inside. There are no vehicles to contend with in there, so anything that's heavily armored and capable of mowing down infantry is king. That would be the MAX.

INTERIOR BASE DEFENDER

Bases need solid defense, and anti-personnel MAXes are ideal for manning the interior portion of the base. They can also be very useful in the courtyard or around the walls, though they're more vulnerable in open terrain than they are within a base's confines. Outside, they're vulnerable to vehicles and long-range anti-vehicle weapons.

Anti-personnel MAXes are also crucial when you've just hacked an enemy Command Console and must settle in to defend it for 15 minutes.

TASKS FOR THE ANTI-VEHICLE MAX

The anti-vehicle MAX configuration is, as you might expect, particularly good at dealing with enemy vehicles of all descriptions. It's also the best (though not by a huge margin) at destroying other MAXes. This makes the anti-vehicle MAX both fun to play and very useful in a variety of roles.

EXTERIOR BASE ATTACKER

Large-scale assaults tend to involve lots of outdoor fighting. It's important to bring anti-vehicle MAXes along to better deal with enemy MAXes and enemy vehicles.

An assault that doesn't have enough vehicles and anti-vehicle MAXes stands a good chance of failure. That's because the defenders' vehicles and Wall Turrets can rip through infantry with ease. You need strong anti-armor and anti-vehicle capabilities to neutralize those defensive assets, thereby permitting your infantry to get inside the base itself.

EXTERIOR BASE DEFENDER

Anti-vehicle MAXes are useful for all sorts of base defense, but they get the most mileage when they're perched on walkways or roaming the courtyards. If they stay close to pillars, walls, and other pieces of cover, they can use their small size (compared to vehicles) and potent weapons to blast enemy vehicles, yet duck back into cover when injured.

NOTE

Cover is also important if you want to avoid getting squashed. It's easy to forget that vehicles can not only shoot you with their weapons, but also run you over—even when you're in MAX armor.

AMS OR TOWER DEFENDER

A good assault typically requires at least one AMS. Despite your best intentions, your AMS will eventually get discovered—especially if you're participating in a large-scale assault featuring dozens of players. The steady stream of fighters originating from a particular area will give the AMS's position away.

When your foes discover your AMS's position, they'll try to deal with it. Stealth hackers may try to jack the AMS, but it's hard for them to go unnoticed if there are lots of players in the area. Similarly, enemy infantry can usually be handled by the steady stream of players respawning at the AMS.

With that in mind, enemy vehicles and MAXes are biggest threat to your AMS. The friendly infantry fighters spawning at the AMS aren't likely to be a match for Reavers, tanks, or MAX squads. That's why it's nice to have an anti-vehicle MAX (or two) standing guard near the AMS. The anti-vehicle MAX can deal with heavy attackers that would otherwise reduce the AMS to rubble.

The same principle applies when your forces are originating in a tower. Vehicles will eventually come out to deploy infantry, to take down the tower's Wall Turrets, or just to stem the tide of infantry. An anti-vehicle MAX can keep those enemy vehicles at bay.

TASKS FOR THE ANTI-AIR MAX

The anti-air MAX is probably the most specialized MAX, since you'll encounter more infantry and land vehicles than air vehicles in most situations. However, as anyone who's dealt with a squadron of enemy Reavers can attest, aerial attacks can be devastating if you don't have the right gear to defeat them. Anti-air MAXes help reduce aerial units to scrap.

Also, bear in mind that the anti-air MAX is still a capable opponent, even when fighting non-aerial units.

EXTERIOR BASE DEFENSE

It's not uncommon to attack a base with Reavers, in an attempt to soften up the exterior defenses and distract the enemy from the ground attack. In such cases, having gunners in the Wall Turrets helps—and having mobile defense forces helps even more. Anti-air MAXes can harass attackers of all sorts, but they are particularly useful at putting a stop to aerial nuisances.

AMS DEFENSE

As mentioned earlier, the defender is likely to target your AMS during a large-scale assault. Reavers are fast and capable, and are therefore a logical way of taking down these vehicles. Without sound anti-air defenders, the AMS stands little chance of survival. Because of this, it's useful to have allies in anti-air MAXes at the ready.

In fact, anti-air MAXes are generally useful in any base assault—but unlike other troops, who will typically try to penetrate the base itself, the anti-air MAXes may want to hang around the edges of the fight. From semiprotected vantage points, they can hammer aerial forces that threaten to harass and stall the invasion.

GENERAL ANTI-AIR DETERRENCE

If enough opponents decide to fly Mosquitoes and Reavers, the skies can get pretty crowded. As a result, even the simplest task—like getting from a friendly base to an attack zone—becomes a chore.

If this becomes the case, climb into an anti-air MAX and start patrolling the areas where aircraft are thickest. Without a strong deterrent in place, other Empires' would-be Top Guns can make your Empire's commonplace operations a real pain.

GENERAL INFANTRY

If you've decided to be a fighter but you aren't in a MAX, you'll fall into this all-purpose category. The name isn't glamorous, and the armor is nothing compared with that of a MAX, but a wide selection of weapons and tools gives non-MAX fighters a lot of choices.

ANTI-VEHICLE FIGHTERS

Every squad can use a player or three with Anti-Vehicle Weapons Certifications. These squad members are responsible for protecting the squad from MAXes and vehicles while the squad is on foot.

These fighters are in many ways the core of the squad. Why take them instead of anti-vehicle MAXes? The short answer is versatility: They can perform other roles in addition to their vehicle-killing duties. Typically they load up on anti-personnel weapons as well, or learn other useful skills like Repair or Medical. The end result is a more flexible squad than one composed mainly of MAXes.

Anti-vehicle fighters typically carry Phoenixes, Strikers, or Lancers, though they can also carry Decimators or other heavy weapons. Hybrid fighters who want to handle infantry as well, without using excessive inventory space, can take a more general-purpose weapon instead (say, a Chaingun) and pack a good supply of armor-piercing rounds. Reinforced Battle Armor is the armor of choice for this role.

ANTI-PERSONNEL FIGHTERS

Another squad mainstay, anti-personnel fighters typically wear Reinforced Battle Armor and carry heavy-hitting weapons like the Mini-Chaingun, Lasher, or Jackhammer. Other weapon choices are acceptable as well; in fact, medium assault weapons such as the Gauss Rifle tend to be better than the big guns at medium to long range.

To some degree, everyone is an anti-personnel fighter; even players who spend most of their time in combat vehicles will occasionally have to fight on foot. You can get away with just the Medium Assault Weapons Certification, and then diversify, or you can go the whole nine yards and pick Heavy Assault Weapons or Special Assault Weapons as well.

SUPPORT ROLES

The very notion of a "support role" may be put off some players. Who wants to do all the grunt work while others duke it out and revel in the glory?

There are several reasons to perform a support role. One very compelling reason is that support roles make your team more effective. If everyone can shoot a gun, but nobody can drive a vehicle or repair anything, you're not likely to get very far or do very much.

Also, many support roles are secondary roles. Your character can be a fighter and still grab a few support Certifications, effectively performing more than one useful function for the squad.

Finally, support roles can be more fun than fighting. An advanced medic can actually revive dead characters—an extremely powerful and satisfying ability! Engineers can dispatch enemies with well-placed mines and turrets. Drivers can control when and where their squad travels, and drive right over enemies who happen to get in the way.

TRANSPORT OR SUPPORT DRIVER

Drivers are crucial to any squad. AMS drivers lay the foundation for a solid attack. Galaxy pilots, as well as Deliverer and Sunderer drivers, get large groups of soldiers to a target, minimizing casualties and distractions. ANT drivers perform a particularly unglamorous role, but it's necessary; without a constant supply of NTUs, your bases will eventually turn neutral.

Consider taking an AMS Certification or a large vehicle certification if your squads have problems finding a ride, finding an AMS, or restocking friendly facilities with NTUs. The job isn't flashy, but if you're the impatient type you'll appreciate being able to dictate when and where these important vehicles go.

MEDIC

Medics are useful squadmates, especially on assault missions that take you far away from friendly Medical Terminals.

At a minimum, medics all have the Medical Certification, which allows use of the Medical Applicator. Some also have the Advanced Medical Certification; this allows them to heal themselves and others faster, and to revive dead soldiers that have not yet chosen a respawn point. Therefore, it can be useful to wait awhile before picking a respawn point if you know there's a squadmate with the Advanced Medical Certification nearby.

Medic is almost never a full-time (or even a most-time) job; at the very least, medics should also be able to fight. Medics can wear any armor type, though Reinforced Body Armor is typical, as it allows the medic to carry an array of weapons in addition to the medical gear.

NOTE

We don't recommend taking the Advanced Medical Certification unless you're already using your Medical Certification a lot. Considering the easy availability of respawn points during a typical well-planned attack or defense, we don't think reviving fallen squadmates is necessary in most situations.

ENGINEER

Engineering tasks include repairing and deploying objects, and repairing players' armor. These aren't the most glamorous tasks in the game, but they provide a real edge for a squad benefiting from the engineer's services. Consequently, you should strongly consider these skills.

SQUAD MEMBERS WITH REPAIR SKILLS ONLY

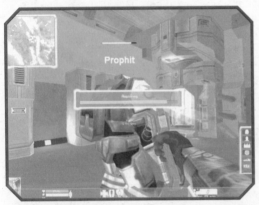

The Repair Certification is the prerequisite for Combat Engineering. It allows the use of the BANK (Body Armor Nanite Kit), which repairs body armor, and the Nano Dispenser, which repairs vehicles and objects.

Repair skills are an excellent adjunct to combat skills. Since the Repair Certification alone is not very Certification-Point intensive, it's possible to easily add Repair skills to a character focused in other areas.

It's useful to have several squad members with Repair Certifications. Their ability to repair body armor is particularly useful in keeping the squad's MAXes in good shape during prolonged missions. (Other players can also benefit from the armor repairs, of course, but MAXes depend so much on their thick armor that repairs are extra-useful for them.)

SQUAD MEMBERS WITH COMBAT ENGINEERING

Most leaders' ideal squad includes at least one member with the Combat Engineering Certification. This skill is necessary for fortifying and maintaining a base when you're playing defense; those Boomer HEs, HE Mines, Spitfire Turrets, and Motion Sensors are part of what gives the defending team its edge.

Having more than two squad members with Combat Engineering skills is probably a bit redundant, as two can pack an awful lot of defensive gear in an SOI.

The bottom line: It's useful to have several squad members with Repair abilities, but only one or two of them need to have Combat Engineering as well.

SCOUT

A scout's job is to figure out what the enemy is doing, and then report back to the squad (and possibly the whole outfit, depending on the situation).

Scouts almost always play other roles as well. Since an Infiltration Suit is the only "must-have" Certification for this role, it's not tough to diversify.

NOTE

While you can try to be a scout without an Infiltration Suit, it's tough. The Infiltration Suit's stealth abilities are a perfect match for the scout's information-gathering skills.

Scouts are also invaluable on both offense and defense. On offense, a scout can separate from the squad and scope out potential target bases; this information can then be used to pick an appropriate target. On defense, scouts can root out enemy AMSes or report on incoming enemies from a position somewhat outside the base's walls.

At higher Battle Ranks, scouts will have enough Certification Points to equip themselves with Wraith four-wheelers. The result is the perfect combination of stealth and mobility for characters that spend lots of time scouting. However, many characters won't want to take it that far; they'll typically only scout for a little while, and then rejoin their squad to perform other roles (often, hacking).

HACKER

Hackers are useful squad members, vital to any good assault. Hacking is also one of the few roles that allow you to be effective on your own.

NOTE

Anyone can hack doors and Command Consoles without Certification. The addition of the Hacking Certification opens up the ability to hack any terminal or vehicle.

1236791349l2

Lone hackers can infiltrate unguarded enemy bases, hack them, and then call for reinforcements to help defend the hack. They can also look for enemy vehicles (especially AMSes) and stealthily hack them, turning an enemy resource into a friendly one. This works even better if the hacker has the AMS Certification and can thus drive away the stolen vehicle.

Hackers in a squad are useful for quickly opening doors and hacking Command Consoles. Just as important, they can hack Vehicle Terminals and Equipment Terminals, giving an attacking force access to all the facilities usually reserved for defenders.

SPECIALIZED COMBAT ROLES

Fighting the enemy doesn't always entail suiting up in heavy armor and slugging it out. Here are a few combat roles that take a decidedly different approach.

SNIPER

Snipers carry a Bolt Driver rifle. They can wear Reinforced Battle Armor or a Light Exosuit (or a Standard Exosuit, though never by choice).

On offense, snipers tend to look for a hilltop near an enemy base. The higher they can get, the better view they have. Once there, they start picking off targets from the walls and the base interior.

NOTE

Sniping on offense can be pointless if there isn't a conventional attack happening as well. Otherwise, the end result is just a sniper battle with no tactical significance.

On defense, snipers tend to wander the base walls and the upper floors of the base itself. Clever snipers may leave the base area entirely and seek high ground, as the attackers won't expect a defensive sniper located far away from the base.

Sniping isn't recommended for beginning characters, as the Bolt Driver demands several Certifications. Also, sniping is usually a solo endeavor, and it's best not to go solo at first; you'll collect BEPs faster by sticking with a squad. Later on, however, you may wish to take up the Bolt Driver and test your skills.

ASSAULT VEHICLE DRIVER

Drivers of transport vehicles and other useful vehicles (like the AMS and ANT) aren't in their vehicles full-time. They usually grab a vehicle, take it somewhere, and then get out.

Assault vehicles like tanks and Reavers are different; their drivers tend to be specialists and can spend the majority of a play session in the cockpit or behind the wheel.

Vehicle specialists don't need to worry about most other Certifications, at least at first. They can grab their chosen vehicle Certification, hop inside a vehicle, and they're good to go. If these players are with a squad, they may leave the vehicle when the squad infiltrates an enemy base—or, they may let the others handle the interior work and simply patrol the base exterior.

Reavers are popular choices for assault vehicle specialists, since they require only a single pilot and are quite effective in combat. Don't forget about large tanks, though. Even light ground vehicles can be deadly if you truly master them and become adept at running people down.

GUNNER

Gunners spend a lot of time in Wall Turrets or in the gunner position of heavy assault vehicles. These players typically have other roles as well, but there are exceptions. A gunner with a friend that consistently drives a Prowler tank, for example, can spend most of the time in that tank.

Gunners' only requirement is a Light Exosuit, since heavier armor types disqualify them from certain gunner positions. Beyond that, they can specialize in any number of other areas.

Beginning characters should look for gunner opportunities, since this is not a Certification-intensive role. Look to hop into Wall Turrets if your squad is playing defense, or jump into squadmates' assault vehicles when the squad is on the move. It's an easy way to command potent firepower and rack up quick BEPs.

STEALTH ASSASSIN

The Infiltration Suit isn't always used for infiltration. Players with this Certification can use it to wreak havoc and score stealthy kills, sometimes even helping the greater war effort as they do so.

On offense, a stealth assassin can sneak inside the base walls and take down defenders. A favorite technique is to sneak onto the walls, where it's easy to take down snipers and other defenders who are concentrating on the targets outside.

Stealth assassins can also tag along with a squad that's attacking a base. When a fight breaks out, there are often opportunities to sneak around behind the distracted enemy and score an easy kill.

On defense, stealth assassins can pick off enemies as they try to unlock base doors or as they make their way along base walls or corridors. Or, they can use Darklight Vision to hunt other stealthy characters, thereby keeping the base safe for allies that are busy fighting conventional battles.

USEFUL ROLE COMBINATIONS

As you play *PlanetSide*, you'll have to decide whether to create a character with a wide array of diverse skills or to specialize heavily in one particular area. Either path is legitimate. It's just a matter of figuring out what you like doing and then taking Certifications that let you do those things well.

The following role combinations are useful and effective, and some of them are very common. These are by no means the only useful role combinations; feel free to create your own.

ANTI-VEHICLE AND ANTI-PERSONNEL FIGHTER

If you like fighting on foot, it's natural to want the ability to fight *everything*. You don't want to shoot infantry but run away from vehicles, or vice versa. You want the tools to deal with anything that comes your way! That's why a natural combination is the anti-vehicle and anti-personnel fighter.

This combination is pretty Certification-intensive. It demands Reinforced Battle Armor, mainly for the inventory space, and it typically includes an Anti-Vehicle Weapons Certification. You can also grab Heavy Assault Weapons, though that's not mandatory.

If you pick this combination, you'll typically carry a heavy anti-vehicle weapon such as a Phoenix, Striker, or Lancer, along with a heavy anti-personnel weapon like a Mini-Chaingun. Depending on the target, you can pull out either gun and be extremely effective.

Alternately, you may want to carry your Empire's medium assault weapon instead of a heavy assault weapon. For example, if you're New Conglomerate, you might carry the Gauss instead of the Jackhammer. Doing this would allow you to be effective at longer ranges and would free you from spending Certification Points on Heavy Assault Weapons Certification.

COMBAT ENGINEER

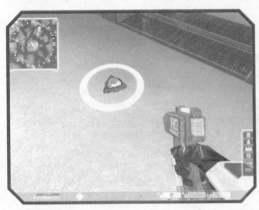

At minimum, combat engineers need the Engineering Certification; many possess Advanced Engineering as well. Additionally, they usually have the Medium Assault Weapons Certification, and maybe some advanced weapon Certifications thrown in for good measure. The result is a good fighter who can heal everyone's armor between battles. This is invaluable when your squad raids an enemy base or fights out in the open, where Medical Terminals are unavailable.

Combat engineers can also fix broken base gear and deploy mines and turrets (if they have Combat Engineering Certification). The result is a satisfying character who can fight effectively and contribute substantially to the defense of a base.

STEALTH HACKER AND MAX

The stealth hacker is a very common, natural character type. Armed with an Infiltration Suit and superb hacking skills, a spy can hack terminals, jack enemy vehicles, scout the terrain, and even get in a few sneaky kills.

But what if you add a MAX to that hacker's Certification list? Now you have someone who can infiltrate an enemy base, hack it, hack an Equipment Terminal, and then switch into powerful MAX armor to assist with the defense.

Stealth hackers and MAXes play very dissimilar roles, but you should never underestimate the value of being able to freely switch between them.

STEALTH ENGINEER

A character with Combat Engineering Certification and an Infiltration Suit can't carry much gear. However, there's enough inventory room in an Infiltration Suit for a few ACE devices.

This may not be the most practical combination, but it's one of the most wickedly funny. Sneak into an enemy base unseen, drop a Boomer, and then detonate it while your unsuspecting targets wonder what happened. Or, use multiple Boomers to destroy valuable base equipment (like a Generator).

On defense, prowl the base courtyard and drop Spitfire Turrets right next to infiltrators. Watch the Spitfire light them up; they'll wonder how they missed it! Or, sneak up to an enemy AMS and drop Spitfires in a ring around it. Confusion and mayhem are bound to ensue.

MULTIPLE VEHICLE SPECIALIST

You can forgo the whole infantry experience and take multiple vehicle Certifications. With no need to spend Certification Points on weapons or armor, you can master several vehicles and be assured of having the right vehicle for every situation.

For example, you could master the AMS, Galaxy, and MagRider. Now you have the power to lay the foundation for an attack, move around a whole squad, or patrol an area in a deadly vehicle. You're versatile and useful to your team, and you always have something to do.

MORE COMBINATIONS

Take any combination of Certifications that interest you, and play any combination of roles you enjoy. Make a few concessions to your Empire's needs or your squad's needs—for example, if there's always a chronic shortage of AMS drivers, consider taking that Certification. But don't take it if you really hate driving an AMS; stick to the things you like, as you're likely to be better at them.

Do pay attention to other players' roles, because it can lead to opportunities. If you're constantly deluged by stealth hackers, grab the Darklight Vision Implant and appoint yourself a hacker hunter. If swarms of Reavers cloud the skies, consider taking an Anti-Vehicle Weapons Certification and feasting on all the targets. Your role is always most useful and entertaining if it directly counters an activity lots of players are engaged in.

CHAPTER 11: ADVANCED PLAY

Once you've learned all the basics, focus on refining and improving your skill level. This chapter offers suggestions on a wide array of topics, including squad composition, effective AMS use, getting the most out of your deployable items, and more. The common thread: It's all geared toward making you a more effective *PlanetSide* player.

THE IDEAL SQUAD?

There's no such thing as an ideal or perfect squad. However, certain mixtures of Certifications and player roles work better than others.

POOR SQUAD COMPOSITION: AMUSING, BUT NOT HELPFUL

Imagine a full squad composed only of hackers in Infiltration Suits. It would certainly be fun, and very annoying to the enemy: Picture the hacker squad swarming a hostile base, unlocking every door, hacking Equipment Terminals and Vehicle Terminals, and stabbing lightly armored guards in the back at every opportunity.

But could our intrepid hacker squad stand up to a well-organized, diversified opposition? The answer, clearly, is no. After a short while the defenders would figure out what was going on, and they'd be extra-vigilant. Worse, a single defender with Darklight Vision could mow down the whole squad!

Even if the defenders failed to destroy the hacker squad outright, the hackers could not take over the base. They could sneak in and hack the Command Console, but the defenders would march in a MAX or three and a hacker of their own, and take it right back. The MAXes would protect the defenders' hacker, and there's not a thing the hacker squad could do about it (assuming, of course, a basic level of competence on the defenders' behalf).

Now imagine the other end of the spectrum: a whole squad populated entirely with MAXes. This squad could wreak havoc, especially if members confined their activity to a spot with good respawn facilities.

But the downside of this squad becomes apparent when it needs to do something besides fight. If the MAXes attack an enemy base, they…get stuck at the front door, because nobody can hack open the simple lock. If they're playing defense and the Generator gets destroyed, nobody can fix it. If the nearby AMS is destroyed or stolen, they can't drive in a new one.

As you can see, an unbalanced squad can be very effective under certain limited circumstances—but outside those circumstances it becomes helpless. Strive for a more balanced squad.

NOTE

You can sometimes get away with an unbalanced squad in a large-scale battle, because other squads are likely to provide the skills your squad is missing. It's a lot tougher when your squad is on its own.

SQUAD COMPOSITION: A GOOD MODEL

The designers recommend the following model squad for general-purpose combat. It's not perfect for every situation, but it's an excellent starting point:

- *Two MAXes:* Usually these are both anti-personnel MAXes, or one anti-personnel and one anti-vehicle.

- *Two Heavy Assault Soldiers:* These players typically wear reinforced armor and carry tough anti-personnel weapons.

- *Two Anti-Vehicle Soldiers:* These squad members are like the heavy assault soldiers, but they carry weapons geared toward destroying vehicles and MAXes.

- *Two Medics/Engineers:* During combat, these squad members help with the fight (although they stay back); between battles they heal teammates' health and armor, revive fallen comrades, and deploy ACE combat devices.
- *Two Hackers:* At least one hacker (and maybe both) should be in an Infiltration Suit. They open doors, hack vital terminals, steal enemy vehicles, and act as scouts.

Mix and match these skills. For example, heavy assault soldiers are often anti-vehicle soldiers as well. It's assumed that various team members will possess other crucial skills, such as the ability to drive an AMS and assorted combat vehicles. A squad with no vehicles is very limited.

These guidelines should not be viewed as immutable. This is just a good model for a versatile, effective squad that can attack bases, defend bases, or do anything else demanded of it.

Also, even if you're trying to follow this model very closely, it's fine to alter the mix. Having more than two MAXes, for example, can be very effective when the bullets start flying.

NOTE

If at least one member of the squad can fly a Galaxy, and another can drive an AMS, you're well prepared for most combat duties. You'll need more vehicle skills than that if you plan to do lots of outdoor fighting, however.

SPECIALIZED SQUADS FOR SPECIALIZED DUTY

If your squad is going to perform a very specialized task, it can be helpful to mix up the team members and load up on certain Certifications/weapons/armors/skills.

For example, if your squad's main goal is to interfere with enemy attacks *before* they get to your facilities, jettison the MAXes. Instead, try using hackers in Infiltration Suits and combat vehicle drivers. The hackers can scout and jack enemy vehicles, while the drivers can intercept enemy vehicles and destroy them—preferably far away from your base.

If your plan is to hunker down on defense in a friendly base, get rid of the dedicated hackers and replace them with MAXes. After all, you don't need to hack very much when you already own everything. If the enemy manages to hack the base, you'll have to re-hack it—but any non-MAX with a Remote Electronics Kit is capable of that, given enough time.

REALITY INTERFERES

Unless you have a very dedicated core group that shows up at regular times, and everybody plans character development according to the group's needs, reality will interfere with your carefully laid plans. You won't always get the skill sets, armor, and weapons you want.

Ultimately, your group is determined by who is available and what those people can do. Don't fret, though; everybody has the same problem. If you set a target for the skills, armor types, and weapon types you want in your squad, and you proceed with that target in mind, you'll be way ahead of many opponents.

THINGS TO AVOID

Everyone makes mistakes. The interesting thing about *PlanetSide* is that you can get killed a lot and still be a very effective player. Or, you can slay legions of foes and not make much difference at all. Here are a few tips on avoiding the most common pitfalls.

AVOIDING POINTLESS BATTLES

We guarantee that some folks won't understand the goals of *PlanetSide*, no matter how long they play. Instead of engaging in important activities, like attacking or defending a base, they'll wade into pointless battles and consistently fail to help their Empire.

You'll always be able to find pointless battles, no matter where you look. These battles often take place outside, halfway between an attacking force's AMS and a defending base (or between an attacking tower and defending base). Attackers continuously respawn at the AMS, trickle out onto the plains, and start running around and shooting at base defenders that have likewise trickled out from the base walls.

This sort of fighting can be futile. The defenders mow down the attackers like wheat, but the attackers keep popping up at that AMS. On the flip side, the attackers keep shooting the defenders wandering through the area, but they'll never get inside the base itself.

NOTE

It's fine to engage in pointless fights when you first start to play. This sort of continual action helps you rack up BEPs and gain Battle Ranks. When you've reached a comfortable Battle Rank, though, it's time to start thinking more strategically.

In this situation, the defenders are "winning," since the attackers probably won't get anywhere—but they could still do better. They should gather some combat vehicles or mass in overwhelming numbers and go take out that AMS or tower. Then, blasting the attackers will actually *mean* something; they'll respawn farther away, and they'll have to waste lots of time and effort to get back.

Likewise, the attackers need to gather near the AMS, then advance on the base as a group; ideally they should head for the back door, so they can avoid as much fighting on the base grounds as possible. Meanwhile, a driver should hang back and drive the AMS to a safer location.

NOTE

If you find yourself fighting near a tower or AMS, and you never seem to be getting any closer to the enemy base, either call in reinforcements for a big push or rethink your strategy and try another tactic or location.

THE LONELY SNIPER

Snipers are often the target of derision. They're seen as useless and annoying fighters, capable of dishing out cheap shots but never really affecting the game. On the other hand, if they're good enough, they often *do* affect the game—which makes them all the more hated.

Snipers in *PlanetSide* are somewhat less versatile than those in other multiplayer action games. They're limited by the single-action nature of the Bolt Driver, and even more so by the nature of the battlefields.

Battlefields are huge, and all the critical stuff is inside the actual bases. Offensive sniping is pointless if there's nobody on the walls or within direct view of the base's main entrance; meanwhile, defensive sniping is often less effective than climbing into a Wall Turret.

There *is* a useful role for sniping in *PlanetSide*. Heavily defended bases with enemies patrolling the walls and manning the gun turrets can be very hard to breach with an all-out charge; an offensive sniper can help soften up the defenses or distract defenders from the main assault.

Likewise, a defensive sniper on the base walls can sometimes pick off a few members of an incoming squad, such that it disrupts the squad's cohesiveness.

The bottom line is that sniping can be tactically useful, but only if nearby teammates are mounting a traditional attack or defense as well. If that's not happening, abandon the sniper's post.

THE COMPRESSED DEFENSE

It's easy to get into ultra-defensive mode while on defense. In this mode, everyone packs down into the basement (or up into the top floor) near the Command Console and waits.

This method is effective to a point, but if everyone's gathered at the Command Console you lose a lot of your base's advantages. There's nobody manning the Wall Turrets, nobody looking for the enemy AMS in an Infiltration Suit, nobody buying tanks and driving them around the base, mowing down invaders that get caught along the way.

Remember that the best defenses make attackers worry about what's outside the base. If you let your opponents get inside your base with no resistance, you've already given up much of your edge.

THE ALL-IMPORTANT AMS

It is not an exaggeration to state that the AMS (Advanced Mobile Station) is the key to most successful base assaults. While your assault *can* succeed without an AMS, your chances of success are greatly reduced if you aren't making use of this important vehicle.

As discussed in chapter 4, an AMS is a vehicle that provides both Respawn Tubes and an Equipment Terminal. Effectively, it duplicates the two most crucial functions of a friendly base.

Consider an assault on a remote enemy base. Your squad penetrates the outer defenses, wins its way into the basement, and sustains heavy losses. Despite the losses, a lone hacker manages to get to the Command Console and hack it for your side.

Now what? If you brought along an AMS and parked it just outside the base, fallen squad members will be able to respawn there, grab appropriate gear for defending the hacked console (a few anti-personnel MAXes might be nice…), and get right back into the action. You'll need them, because that hacker can't defend the Command Console alone.

What if there's no AMS nearby? Fallen squad members reappear in the closest friendly tower or facility, which could be halfway across the continent! Even if it's not, the time required to get from wherever they appeared to the base you're assaulting is prohibitive. By the time they're back, the enemy has likely mopped the floor with your poor little hacker and re-hacked the Command Console. All your effort was wasted, and you're back at square one.

DEMAND AN AMS

If you're on a squad that's about to attack without an AMS, don't be afraid to stick your hand in the air and say, "Hey, where's the AMS?" Unless there's a really good reason not to bother with one (e.g., you know for a fact that the target base is empty, and you're confident you can hold off the counterattack), always bring one.

It's possible to mount a good attack from a tower instead of an AMS, but an ideal attack originates from more than one place. It's best to have *both* a tower and AMS in the vicinity.

NOTE

In situations where getting an AMS into the area quickly is impractical, have someone lag behind and drive one in while the rest of the squad performs a covert attack.

HIDING AN AMS

A deployed AMS creates a cloaking dome that hides it from enemies—except for those that get really close. This is a powerful tool, and it's also necessary. AMSes are crucial, so smart enemies will place a high priority on their destruction. The best defense is preventing the enemy from knowing they're there.

How can you keep your AMS a secret? Here are some recommendations:

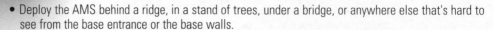

- Deploy the AMS behind a ridge, in a stand of trees, under a bridge, or anywhere else that's hard to see from the base entrance or the base walls.

- Send a scout in an Infiltration Suit ahead to report back on the status of the base. If the walls and the area around the base are manned with enemies, deploy the AMS farther from the base than you usually would.

- Be careful not to accidentally un-deploy the vehicle when you mean to access the Equipment Terminal. It's easy to do, and the cloaking shield drops when the vehicle isn't deployed.

- When you're near the enemy base, avoid roads if at all possible. You're more likely to be seen there, because of enemy traffic, and it's an obvious route.

- Avoid approaching the enemy base from the obvious route. For example, if your Empire's only nearby tower or base is due south of your target, park your AMS to the north. Now you can easily attack from both directions.

- Don't stand around the AMS, and don't fight near it unless it's clear that it's already been discovered. Nothing is a bigger tip-off to an AMS than a bunch of soldiers milling around in a particular area.

- If the AMS *is* discovered, defend it and then drive it away. A lot of players never think to do this, but you should; once the AMS's location is common knowledge, its days are definitely numbered.

It's easy to dismiss these tips as simple common sense, and for the most part they are—but it's surprising how many players don't heed them in the heat of battle.

For example, we've seen many cases where squad members spawn at an AMS, equip themselves, and then start shooting at a distant enemy that has no idea where the AMS is. Never do that! Get away from the AMS before fighting. The same goes for sniping; don't grab a Bolt Driver and hunker down near the AMS! It just draws unwanted attention to the area.

PROTECTING AN AMS

When you spawn at an AMS, don't blindly grab your gear and run away. Take a quick look outside the dome of invisibility and make sure there isn't an enemy force bearing down on you. Also look around inside the dome. Activate your Darklight Vision if you have it. There may be a hacker in an Infiltration Suit jacking the AMS right out from under your nose!

After your brief inspection, feel free to go about your business. If and when the enemy does attack the AMS, defend it at all costs. If you're killed, choose to respawn to that AMS and hope that your teammates can defend it until you reappear.

When you do reappear, don't skimp on equipment (unless the enemy is a fragile hacker). Run to the Equipment Terminal at the back of the vehicle, quickly select your heaviest fighting package (you *did* pre-assign several inventory packages, didn't you?), and beat down the attackers.

If you defeat all nearby foes, pack up the AMS and drive it to a new location.

YOU CAN NEVER HAVE TOO MANY AMSES

Two AMSes are usually better than one. Three AMSes are excellent for a big, multi-squad invasion.

The question with the AMS is always: How close to the target should I bring it? The closer you get, the more convenient and efficient it is—but the more likely it is to be discovered and destroyed. Bringing multiple vehicles, however, makes the decision easier. If you have more than one AMS, you can take some chances that you might not otherwise take.

When you have multiple AMSes, leave one AMS back in a safe location and bring another one to a riskier, more convenient spot. You can even have a chain of several AMSes, so that if one gets destroyed you'll always have another one handy.

Is it possible to bring too many AMSes? Generally, that's not a concern. The one real exception is when enemy hackers are aggressively scouting for AMSes, with the sole intent of jacking them. If you have a small invasion force but a lot of AMSes in the area, several will be deserted for much of the time. An empty AMS is usually unguarded, and it's very easy to jack.

NOTE

Again, we stress that having too many AMSes in an area is, at worst, a minor problem. Worry more about not having any at all!

You can't deploy multiple AMS right next to each other; they have a lock-out radius, much like deployed Engineer devices. Also, you can't deploy an AMS too close to a Vehicle Terminal, as this might interfere with the purchase of subsequent vehicles.

HOW CLOSE IS TOO CLOSE?

It's easy to get excited and drive the AMS too close to the enemy base, without knowing how many defenders are there and how likely you are to be seen. If you don't have a scout or an intelligence report, stay back and play it safe. A functional AMS several hundred yards from the base wall is much better than a destroyed AMS within throwing distance.

NTU LEVELS AND ASSAULTS

When planning an assault, definitely take the target base's NTU levels into consideration.

Instead of attacking an enemy base that's down to 10 or 20 percent of its NTU maximum, consider waiting for the NTUs to run out. If they do, the facility will turn neutral, and you'll have a much easier time rooting out the defenders.

If the defenders are competent, though, they'll have sent someone out for an ANT (Advanced Nanite Transport). Stake out an ambush along the roads leading into the base, and get out your anti-vehicular weapons. Watch for ANTs (and Galaxies, since Galaxies can carry ANTs). When the ANT or Galaxy arrives, destroy it. Then, don't assault the base until it goes neutral.

NOTE

Waiting for the ANT only works if you have enough squad members with anti-air and anti-vehicle weapons. Galaxies in particular are very durable, and you'll need several squad members firing simultaneously to take one down.

NOTE

If you're attacking a base that's low on NTUs, one trick is to bring two AMSes and one ANT along for the siege. Deploy one of the AMSes farther from the base than the other, and hide the ANT under its cloaking dome. Then, when you've hacked the facility, drive the ANT in for a quick refueling.

DEALING WITH LIMITED ATTACK RESOURCES

One of the main disadvantages that attackers face is their limited access to vehicles and MAXes. While defenders typically have access to Vehicle Terminals, and Equipment Terminals that allow MAXes, attackers have no such facilities. AMSes don't allow purchases of MAX armor, and there is no mobile equivalent to the Vehicle Terminal.

This is not a major concern in a commando-style raid, where resistance is light enough that everyone can sneak through the facility's back door and take the defenders by surprise. It becomes a major issue, though, during a pitched battle for control of a facility.

Here are a few ways to compensate for your limited resources when you launch a major offensive.

TAKE NEARBY TOWERS

Since you can create MAXes at tower Equipment Terminals, capture a nearby tower and hold it—even if you already have an AMS in a more convenient spot. That way, players who want MAXes can bind there and get into the fight without too much delay.

LOAD UP ON ANTI-VEHICLE WEAPONS

The defenders' vehicles, MAXes, and turrets are a major advantage. You can partially counter this if you have lots of players with anti-vehicle weapons. Five to 10 players with Striker or Phoenix missiles, or the Lancer anti-vehicle laser, can take down Wall Turrets, vehicles, and other heavily armored threats in no time flat.

TRASH THE BASE AS QUICKLY AS POSSIBLE

Make a concerted effort to take down the enemy's Vehicle Terminals, Equipment Terminals, and Generator. Use kamikaze attacks in heavy vehicles, stealthy engineers who deploy Boomers, and anything else you can think of to damage those resources. Without them, a seemingly invincible base will suddenly become vulnerable.

MOVE IN PACKS

Defenders are packed into the area they're trying to defend; this means they tend to cluster into groups, even if they aren't trying to. It's much easier to get scattered and separated on offense, on the other hand, as players trickle out of AMSes or towers and sprint toward the enemy base.

Make a concerted effort to wait for allies to gather, and then move forward in bunches. It's a fundamental point, but it's easy (even for seasoned veterans) to forget it in all the excitement.

MAXIMIZE DEPLOYABLE POWER

Motion Sensors, Spitfire Turrets, and HE Mines (and to a lesser degree, Boomers) are an important part of a solid base defense. Here are a few tips for making sure these items are effective.

USE COVER

Don't place Spitfire Turrets or Motion Sensors where they can be seen from a long distance (and, therefore, destroyed from far away). Place them inside base walls, behind blast shields or exterior bunkers, or behind tree trunks. Anything that prevents incoming enemies from seeing the devices from afar is useful.

AIM HIGH

Spitfire Turrets must be placed on level surfaces, but that doesn't mean they have to go on the ground. Placing them on base walls, on ledges, or on top of the infantry bunkers outside some bases gives them a great vantage point and makes them harder to notice.

Motion Sensors can be placed on inclined surfaces, so you have even more options when placing them. Be creative; place them in spots that are either hard to see or hard to accurately reach with short-range weapons.

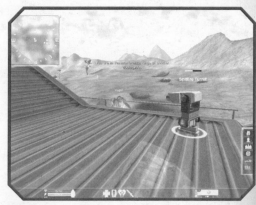

USE CAMOUFLAGE

Place HE Mines near rocks, in tall grass, or behind the doors at the top or bottom of exterior stairwells. Any sort of little blemish or imperfection on the ground can help conceal a mine.

Place Spitfire Turrets and Motion Sensors next to large objects or base features, like Wall Turrets or the base of an exterior Vehicle Terminal. Opponents will often see the large features but not the turrets and sensors.

TIP

Placing Spitfire Turrets right in front of Wall Turrets is a useful trick. Opponents will assume that the Wall Turret is firing at them, when it's really the Spitfire.

GROUP EXPLOSIVES WITH OTHER ITEMS

Hide mines and Boomers behind Spitfire Turrets. If sneaky opponents try to creep up and destroy the Spitfire, they'll get a nasty surprise.

CAUTION

Be careful not to place your explosives too close to permanent base objects, such as friendly Wall Turrets or Vehicle Terminals.

STEALTH TECHNIQUES

Infiltration Suits are a big part of the game, whether you like them or not. Even if you don't plan to sneak around in one, learn the tricks of the trade so you know what to expect from the players that do.

PATIENCE!

A walking or crouch-walking player in an Infiltration Suit can be seen with the naked eye, but it's difficult. Most stealth players get caught running, as they're quite visible while on the run.

When wearing an Infiltration Suit, run when you're outdoors and there's nobody around. Also run for short periods when you're indoors and quite sure you're alone. Walk or crouch-walk as you approach corners and junctions, or any place where you can't tell if enemies are nearby.

If you have a particular goal in mind (say, destroying a Generator with Boomers, or hacking a Command Console), pass up a few easy kills. Sure, you could shoot that guy at the Equipment Terminal in the back— but if you want to remain unnoticed, that might not be the best idea.

Take it slow and easy when playing the infiltration game. Any other way, and you're likely to get gunned down.

AVOID OBVIOUS PLACES

The Darklight Vision Implant shows all cloaked enemies within a medium radius, but it drains Stamina, and nobody uses it all the time. Typically, players flick it on when they suspect there's an infiltrator nearby, or when they're looking at an area that's especially likely to contain an infiltrator.

Such areas include the main entrance to a base, the area around the Command Console, and the area near the base's back door. As a stealthy player you need to get through those areas as quickly as possible without being noticed. Don't linger; opponents are likely to catch you with their Darklight Vision if you stay in such obvious spots.

DON'T PANIC

Infiltrators face dozens of tense situations every time they invade enemy territory. Did that player down the hallway spot you, or is he walking in your direction for another reason? It can be hard to figure out your opponents' motives.

If an opponent moves directly toward you, the worst thing you can do is panic and move out of the way. That practically guarantees you'll be seen. If there's still some doubt about whether you're visible, just hang tight. If you're wrong and you *were* spotted, the enemy gets an easy kill—which is fine, that's just a risk you take. But many opponents won't notice you if you're crouching motionless—even if they bump into you as they pass.

LET YOUR DARKLIGHT SHINE

When you're a sneaky infiltrator, your worst enemies are often other sneaky types. They tend to use Darklight Vision and be very aware of other stealthy players.

Keep an eye out for other infiltrators, making heavy use of your own Darklight Vision (if you've got it). Killing enemies in Infiltration Suits is often crucial to keeping your cover intact.

KNOW WHEN TO QUIT

Every infiltrator has had the experience of being caught and gunned down, respawning nearby, and then trying it again—only to be caught and gunned down a second time. It happens to everyone.

While a few bad stealth missions are par for the course, after a certain point give it up. Try infiltrating a different base, or switch to a non-stealth package and fight conventionally for a while. If defenders kill enough stealth players in a short time span, they become hyper-sensitive and hyper-alert. That makes it extra hard to get anywhere inside the base. Do yourself a favor and try something else!

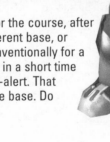

CONTINUED IMPROVEMENT

PlanetSide will continue to grow and evolve as the months go by. Weapon stats may be tweaked, game mechanics may be altered (perhaps drastically), and new facets may be added to the game's overarching strategy. This book can't predict those changes, but we'll leave you with a few tips on the subject of getting better.

STUDY YOUR FAILURES

It's tempting to respawn as quickly as possible every time you're gunned down. That may be good for your ego, but it's bad for your performance. Many times you'll be killed unexpectedly, and if you don't do a little investigating, the circumstances of your unfortunate demise will remain a mystery.

If you aren't sure what got you, look at the chat window and review the kill message. It shows the name of the player that got you (if any) and a picture of the weapon that was used. It's important to figure out whether it was a Wall Turret or a Repeater, a Lightning tank or a Striker. Learning what sort of weapon got you helps you figure out where the attacker was, and what you need to pay more attention to next time. Figuring this stuff out is how you learn and improve! Chalking the kill up to bad luck, on the other hand, is a surefire path to mediocrity.

TEAM UP WITH THE BEST

Figure out who's best in your outfit, and try to join those skillful players' squads. You'll learn much more from following skilled squad leaders than from hanging around with average players. Subtle tricks and techniques will develop as players become ever more familiar with *PlanetSide*, and you can't be expected to figure them all out for yourself. Learn from others, and you'll stay well ahead of the curve.

ACKNOWLEDGE YOUR LIMITATIONS

No matter how skilled you become, *PlanetSide* is still a game of teamwork. If you're used to dominating at games, you may become frustrated at your inability to do so here—even if you're actually a very good player. If you fail to accomplish a particular goal, step back and evaluate your strategy. Consider bringing more allies on board. It's easy to fall into the trap of thinking you should win just because you're better than your opponents. You may be, but you still need good teammates—sometimes, lots of them—to win the toughest battles.